G000277454

'If ever a book of hope like this were need

Rev Richard Fothergill, Founder & C

'*Losing Liberty, Finding Freedom* is a reminder and a loud bright celebration of the power and goodness of God. It traces a journey of faith and loudly exalts in the power of love. I recommend it to anyone who, regardless of their stage of understanding the evil forces ranged against us, is aware of a stirring inside.

This book is much more meaningful to me today than it could possibly have been just four years ago. Between then and now, I have become aware of a dark evil in the world and at the same time, have re-made my connection to God.

Together, we will prevail over evil. Please do not ignore the still, small voice. Let it express itself through your truth-telling, even if to begin with, the audience is only you and a mirror.

Telling the truth renders you immediately more powerful and a force for good in the world. Ultimately, I believe this is how and why we will win, but I implore you to please play your part, to the best of your abilities.

I recommend that you read this book!'

> *For our struggle is not against flesh and blood, but against the rulers, against the powers, against the world forces of this darkness, against the spiritual forces of wickedness in the heavenly places.*
> **(Ephesians 6:12)**

Mike Yeadon, ex Vice President and Worldwide Head of Research into Allergies and Respiratory Diseases, Pfizer UK

'Your book is so natural, your voice, gospel-centred accessible and unpretentious! Such a joy to read. And it shows how obediently and closely you walk with the Lord. It's Word and Spirit! Glory to God!'

KIRSTIE WAINWRIGHT, co-leader of Cheshire Filling Station, UK

'The last few years have seen experts in all walks of life call out harmful policies, failed leadership and corruption. Those of us who have been paying attention have witnessed evil in many forms. Laura has viewed what has happened through her own lens both as a midwife and a Christian.

Losing Liberty, Finding Freedom helps make sense of this by taking us on a journey across the world, and through time, offering readers a pathway to find solace, understanding, and perhaps a roadmap to a future with God'.

DR CLARE CRAIG BM BCH FRCPATH, Diagnostic Pathologist
& Co-Chair of HART (Health Advisory and Recovery Team)

'In the midst of all of the cultural, political and religious challenges to the Gospel today Laura has written a book that will put strength in your veins and cause your spirit to rise up with faith and hope.

Full of inspiring stories from her own life and church history that give examples of how to be led by the Spirit and lead courageous lives that refuse to "conform to the pattern of this world" (Romans 12:2).

This is a call to resist and live in the freedom Jesus has won for us'.

REVD CANON JOHN MCGINLEY, Leader of the Myriad
church planting initiative

'*Losing Liberty, Finding Freedom* is a book aimed at the people of today, who need to be free from the thinking and influences of this world. It is an inspiration, or more an injection, for those who need to be freed from spirit forces that push them to walk in a falsehood and to not see the truth as it is. Laura sheds light on situations that seem hopeless but points to Jesus who is the answer to these problems that exist in society in Sweden, and large parts of the world.

I think the book is highly topical. Many people in the church have slumbered and need to be awakened again. It is a mixture of testimonies and deep insights that liberate and give hope. Laura points to really burning issues that need to be highlighted. A clear Jesus focus with a lot of humor!

As the reader, you will live and step into the freedom Jesus Christ reveals in this book, take it to heart and ponder'.

STEFAN BÖRJESSON, pastor and preacher,
leader of Filling Station Gothenburg, Sweden

Liberty Hill Publishing
555 Winderley Pl, Suite 225
Maitland, FL 32751
407.339.4217
www.libertyhillpublishing.com

Paperback ISBN-13: 978-1-66288-613-3
Ebook ISBN-13: 978-1-66288-614-0

For all the Freedom Warriors and Truth Tellers in this spiritual war.

To the *ekklesia.*

God is spirit, and those who worship Him must worship in spirit and truth
John 4:24 (New American Standard Version)

LOSING LIBERTY
FINDING
FREEDOM

Laura Brett

LIBERTY HILL PUBLISHING

ACKNOWLEDGEMENTS

I never planned to write and publish a book, but I think it was planned for me.

My deep thanks and gratitude goes to the whole team at Liberty Hill Publishing for their support, expertise and encouragement; a special mention to Michael Caryl, Mackenzie Curry and Kim Small for their friendship, support, expertise and guidance throughout.

I also want to pay tribute to those who have spurred me on: Kirstie, Adele, Amanda and Rob, who between them all, have helped me craft this book to be the best it can be and make a greater impact for the Kingdom of God. Thank you.

I would like to thank my darling children for their continuous love, and my husband, Rob, for being my biggest advocate and protector and allowing me to share with the readers some of his own story of pain and transformation.

I would also like to mention dear Julia who interceded and believed in me enough to sow a seed offering almost two years before this book was birthed and I am grateful for the whole Filling Station staff team who cheer me on and enable me to flourish in all that I do as an evangelist and ambassador for Christ.

And finally, but most importantly, I give all my praise to my Lord and Saviour, Jesus Christ who gloriously saved me as a young teenager and who has appointed me and anointed me for such a time as this.

I know I would be nothing without Him and I humbly kneel at his feet in gratitude, awe, praise and worship.

I can do all things through Him who strengthens me
(Philippians 4:13)

CONTENTS

FOREWORD by Rev Richard Fothergill xiii

INTRODUCTION xv

CHAPTER 1: Harrogate, North Yorkshire 1

CHAPTER 2: Dartmouth, Devon 9

CHAPTER 3: Plymouth, Massachusetts 17

CHAPTER 4: Southend-on-Sea, Essex 27

CHAPTER 5: Martha's Vineyard, Massachusetts 33

CHAPTER 6: Chatham, Massachusetts 41

CHAPTER 7: Newport, Rhode Island 47

CHAPTER 8: Long Beach, New York 57

CHAPTER 9: New York City, New York 69

CHAPTER 10: Washington, D.C. 83

CHAPTER 11: The Historical Triangle 91

CHAPTER 12: Wintergreen, Virginia 99

CHAPTER 13: Virginia Beach, Virginia 107

CHAPTER 14: Boston, Massachusetts 113

CHAPTER 15: Leiden, the Netherlands 125

CHAPTER 16: Harrogate, North Yorkshire 127

CHAPTER 17: Jerusalem, Israel. 139

CHAPTER 18: The Nations, the World. 143

PICTURES 150

BIBLIOGRAPHY. 179

FOREWORD

Laura Brett is a dynamic, anointed and unique woman. This book, her first, challenges, entertains, stimulates and comforts in equal measure. Her authentic, winning character comes out in every chapter and it is a text which is hard to put down.

Covering her recent years in medicine and ministry, Laura highlights and articulates well the extraordinary times we are living in, from an honest, faithful Christian perspective. If ever a book of hope like this were needed, it is now as so many of the 'old certainties' of the Western World have been shaken and in some places collapsed completely.

In Britain, all the institutions we have respected for so long have come under critical scrutiny and have often been found wanting. The organised Church, the Monarchy, our Parliament, the NHS, education, media, the police and even the very notion of what it is to be British have been attacked and criticised for many decades, so people's trust and confidence in the future has been undermined.

The same is generally true for other nations in the West and it reflects a wider, invisible battle between good and evil for the soul of nations. I believe much of this 'shaking' is God ordained, in order to push us back to the only sure foundation for any life—the salvation to be found in Jesus Christ. Plus, a society built on the truth of God's revealed principles—through the Jewish people, Jesus and the scriptures.

The Christian story is all about hope, life, truth and a future assured through a relationship with God. Laura describes this reality so well, and with humour and I can heartily recommend this book to you.

REV RICHARD FOTHERGILL
Founder & CEO of the Filling Station Trust

INTRODUCTION

There is an entire generation searching for God.

Lonnie Frisbee

Aboard Flight DL259, Amsterdam Schipol to Boston Logan International Airport

It's remarkable what goes through your mind when cruising 40,000 feet up above the clouds with the world looking so peaceful and beautiful below.

I often feel much closer to God up here—perhaps I am?

Did I switch off the lights and empty the fridge?

Did I remember to send that birthday card?

Are the dogs ok?

Lord, please keep us safe on this flight and bring us safely into Boston. Amen.

Why is it that there are so many movies to choose from on the inflight entertainment system these days?

You could spend the entire flight trying to decide what to watch.

Despite that choice, as I scroll through, there is only one movie that stands out and grabs my attention: *Jesus Revolution*.

Spearheaded by Lonnie Frisbee, this revival story follows the sudden surge in young people adopting the Christian faith in the 1970s through the freedom hippie movement, first in California, then across the United States and around the world.

I know two, sorry, I mean three, *incredible* people who came to faith through this movement—I am an evangelist after all.

My finger hits "play" without further deliberation.

Oh, Lord, we desperately need another *Jesus Revolution*—on both sides of the pond. As I sit on this full transatlantic flight, I can sense the urgency in my spirit.

I wonder, how many people on here know Jesus as their Lord and Saviour?

And what if, *all of a sudden* . . . No, don't go there. Not now, Laura.

But it's a fair question, right?

"There is an entire generation searching for God."

We are living in extraordinary times.

People of every nation have been through a really difficult and challenging few years, and, maybe, it's not over yet.

There has been so much suffering, division, and confusion.

Our world has been physically, financially, and spiritually shaken up. Many people living in our broken and troubled world (which looks so perfect from 40,000 feet) are feeling lost, without a firm foundation, and huge numbers of non-believers and spiritually awakened souls have been searching for the truth.

But what is truth?

Pontious Pilate, the Roman governor of Judaea who presided at the trial of Jesus and gave the order for His crucifixion, said to Him:

What is truth? **John 18:38**

Jesus said:

> *For this purpose I have been born, and for this I have come into the world: to testify to the truth. Everyone who is of the truth listens to My voice.* **John 18:37**

Jesus is Truth. The gospel message is truth.

For the Bible-believing Christian, speaking truth to power and speaking the truth against the lies in this world is not an optional posture for the few—it's a command for the many.

> And *when you know this truth, the truth will set you free.* **John 8:32**

In order to find truth, sometimes you have to start asking the right questions. I've always asked lots of questions; in fact, when we were dating, my (now) husband used to call me "questions" as a nickname.

But I don't think I have ever asked as many questions as I have since 2020.

I've learned it's good practice to question everything, and I no longer take anything at face value. The enemy is a liar and a deceiver, and God has given us a critical-thinking mind for a reason.

But when trouble and persecution comes along, how will we respond?

When there are multitudes of loud voices and opinions competing for our time and attention, who will we listen to?

Jesus said in **John 10:27**:

> *My sheep hear My voice, and I know them, and they follow Me.*

I look out at the ocean below and ponder for a moment; my heartbeat quickens knowing that many Saints have made this pilgrimage journey before me, from the southern shores of the British Isles to the eastern cape of the North American coastline, across 3,000 miles of the Atlantic Ocean to bring the Good News of Jesus Christ to the people of the New World.

Many were escaping religious persecution.

Many were called to evangelise to the nations.

"You Said," a worship song from the 1990s, comes on through my headphones, and I smile:

You said, your glory will fill the Earth
Like water the sea; You said, lift up your eyes
The harvest is here, the Kingdom is near
You said, ask and I'll give the nations to you
Oh Lord, that's the cry of my heart
Distant shores and the islands will see
Your light, as it rises on us.
(Hillsong Music 1999)

The constant hum of the air conditioning seems to be more apparent than before; I check the time—four and a quarter hours until landing.

I gently put my head back, and I close my eyes. *Give us the nations, Lord.*

Then I heard the voice of the Lord, saying, "Whom
shall I send, and who will go for Us?" Then I
said, "Here am I. Send me!" **Isaiah 6:8**

CHAPTER ONE

And patience produces character, and character produces hope.
Romans 5:4-6

Harrogate, North Yorkshire

I recently read that biblical researchers have estimated that *patience* is mentioned almost seventy times in Scripture. Some passages are direct, such as 1 Corinthians 13:4: *"Love is patient."* Some are explored through wonderful stories, like that of Joseph in Genesis 37, an example of suffering and patience, or Abraham and Sarah in Genesis 17:1-27, both longing for a child.

Patience is a valuable quality in a person and widely spoken of as a virtue; it's the ability to wait for something, which can often be very desirable, without getting angry or upset in the process.

Has the LORD asked you to be patient for anything in your life?

In October 2022, my husband and I were given a prophecy about "going south". This was a very personal word of knowledge, spoken over us publicly by a world-renowned Prophet, at a national Christian conference in England.

It was kind of vague, I know; but often, a prophetic word is merely a signpost to a much greater revelation.

God knows the intricate details of every part of our lives from cradle to grave, but thankfully, He chooses not to reveal it all at once.

As I sat on that transatlantic flight, I couldn't help but wonder if that Word was relatable to this particular trip. We were, of course, physically "going south" (from 59.9921° N/ 1.5418° W to 42.3601° N/ 71.0589° W, to be precise) and continuing to travel further south to 36.8516° N at the far eastern point of the First Landings State Park in Virginia Beach.

But was that "south" enough? What did "going south" even mean?

Sometimes in life, the Holy Spirit drops an idea into your mind that simply will not go away, and travelling the East Coast with our maturing family was one of those moments.

I should really introduce myself.

My name is Laura.

I'm officially middle-aged. *Ouch.*

I am married to the most wonderful man.

I am a mother to three.

I'm a qualified midwife and an advocate of good mental health.

I love Jesus because He first loved me. I want the world to know about Him.

I have been involved with ministry for over two decades, and I love to see people set free, healed, restored and living as the best human beings they can possibly be.

I think all animals are a gift from God, particularly dogs and cats.

I love the mountains and the sea.

I don't like pesto (*Correction: Pesto doesn't like me.*)

And when people say to me, "Laura, what do you do?" I reply, "Well, I'm a wife, a mother, a trained midwife, a co-leader of a thriving local ministry and I am blessed to be involved with a number of projects. I work part-time for two incredible Christian charities, a family retail business and any spare moments I have are spent fighting the biggest medical fraud in recent history."

So, here's the thing: we are British citizens, we live in the United Kingdom and The Lord told us we would be visiting America in 2022.

Only, we couldn't.

I don't think any of us need reminding about the past few years, but in case you missed it, a global pandemic was announced by governmental authorities and the mainstream media around the world in March 2020, causing widespread fear, confusion, and national lockdowns, restricting movement of travel of the people and resulting in the enforcement of all sorts of made-up rules and regulations in an attempt to control an invisible assassin of a virus.

The USA made it a requirement that people could only enter the country upon proof of double vaccination of the mandated mRNA injection.

Nobody was forcing anyone to do this, of course, but the truth remained you couldn't participate fully in society unless you did.

Freedom of choice? Absolutely

Freedom to live like everyone else? Absolutely not.

We had a two-tier medical apartheid for a while.

As a midwife, who had worked as an autonomous practitioner advocating the freedom of choice for pregnant and intrapartum women in her care, this was particularly hard for me to understand. Had the world gone completely mad?

I think it did for a while.

Suffice to say, due to this little immigration legislation, it made things more complicated for us, but we trust in the God of the Impossible.

He makes a way where there is no way.

Amen?

We believe in a God who says:

"Truly I say to you, whoever says to this mountain, 'Be taken up and thrown into the sea,' and does not doubt

*in his heart, but believes that what he says is going to happen, it will be granted to him." **Mark 11:23***

So, we need to respond, "Mountain, move!"

The truth is, we could have gone sooner, but that would have come at a significant cost. God was telling us to be patient, and we had to hold the line.

When we are patient for the things the Lord puts on our heart, trusting God's sovereign timing rather than rushing ahead to do it ourselves with a quick fix or to do it our own way because we're not willing to wait it out—the worldly systems telling us "You can have it now if you just do this"—the Lord blesses us abundantly, and that patience then produces good character and palace training[1] in us that we wouldn't have learned otherwise.

The waiting game is hard and counter-cultural; having patience is not easy – but that's the whole point.

> *We also have joy with our troubles, because we know that these troubles produce patience. **And patience produces character, and character produces hope.** And this hope will never disappoint us, because God has poured out his love to fill our hearts. He gave us his love through the Holy Spirit, whom God has given to us.* **Romans 5:3-5**

Figuratively speaking, we'd been here before as a family, and God, through His infinite wisdom and kindness, has taught us how to be patient in our undesirable circumstances. Patience is a virtue.

It is a fruit of the Holy Spirit and a precious gift that is not exercised enough in this fast-paced, instant results, "must have" culture that we find ourselves living in.

---

[1] Palace training – referring to the story of *Joseph* in Genesis 37-50

You see, when God whispers something to you in the quiet place, when the God of the angel armies has commanded something into being, you better believe it!

We knew we would be going the following year; it was just a question of when.

In order to be a "mountain mover," you've got to have the faith they will move (Matt. 17:20). Sometimes, that means you've got to take that step of faith and ask God to do the rest. For us, that looked like buying five transatlantic air fares, spending thousands of pounds, and knowing full well that we couldn't enter the USA unless they lifted the immigration rules based on medical status.

God is always saying to each and every one of us, "Do you trust Me?"

He said it to Jeremiah:

*"Leave your orphans behind, I will keep them alive; And let your widows **trust in Me.**" **Jeremiah 49:11***

Proverbs 3:5 says:

Trust in the Lord with all your heart. And do not lean on your own understanding.

Our making sense of this whole situation was stolen from us a long time ago, and so, we had no other choice but to trust Him. We prayed, and we booked the tickets, by faith, at the beginning of 2023 with the intention of travelling in late June, and we continued to pray daily and give it to Him.

Prayer should be foundational to everything and is a mighty weapon in the heavenly realms, demolishing strongholds and changing our situations.

Romans 12:12 says this:

Rejoice in hope, be patient in tribulation,
be constant in prayer.

On May 11, 2023, just six weeks before departure, the immigration rules were changed, and we were given an open door to travel.

Very often, God will take you right down to the wire *because* He wants you to trust Him. If the answer was easy or instant, where would the lesson be?

It is in the waiting and in the sometimes-painful lead up that God reveals to you His intentions or wants to reform or transform your character.

When the Lord ordered Abraham to sacrifice his beloved son Isaac at Moriah (Genesis 22), He left it until the last possible moment before intervening. And so, it is with us—so that our pure hearts and clean hands and a healthy fear and love for Him is revealed.

And then, there is the story of Joseph (and his coat of many colours), who went from highly-favoured son to desert slave, to being wrongly accused and imprisoned, to finally, promoted to Pharaoh's second-in-command in the Egyptian palace—but "the Lord was with him" through every stage of his training and prepared him for what was to come (Genesis 37-50).

He is constantly asking all of us:

❖ How much are you willing to lose for this?
❖ How long are you willing to wait?
❖ Will you trust Me?

God is so kind.

Saturday, June 24, 2023 came. The United States of America—here we come!

PS: *God—sorry, it's me again. Just one more thing. Please help me to meet someone who's influential and powerful on this trip; someone I can pray over and ask Jesus to do a great and glorious work in their hearts, and may they come running to the mercy seat of Christ in repentance.*

Amen.

CHAPTER TWO

*Do not participate in the useless deeds of darkness,
but instead even expose them.*
Ephesians 5:11

Dartmouth, Devon

There is usually a story before the main story, and for this, I need to go back to Dartmouth in Dorset in the post-lockdown summer of 2021.

I wonder if, like many people, I've tried to erase from my memory much of the trauma inflicted upon the world in 2021. We had three teenage children at home for months on end, trying to educate themselves over the internet, missing exams, school trips, and many childhood milestone events.

We were locked up in our homes and couldn't visit loved ones.

We were told to wear masks "for our health" and take experimental medication.

Our churches closed their doors.

Human touch was strictly forbidden.

Relationships with friends and family were severed.

Some people grieved alone.

Some people married alone.

Some people died and were buried alone.

It's beyond comprehension now.

Most of the "rules" didn't seem to make any logical sense whatsoever, but the "rules" were still followed by many.

Others attended freedom protests in various cities.

Some spoke out on social media and wrote letters to challenge the status quo.

By the time the summer came, we were ready for a change of scenery, however limited we were to travel. I remember the frenzy of PCR testing in the summer of 2021 and people cancelling their holiday plans at the last minute to "keep others safe for the greater good."

Collectivism had entered the building at an alarming rate.

How can a PCR test for a virus work properly anyway? It didn't.

On the upside, the roads were fairly empty, and the restaurants had unusual availability. It wasn't all bad.

We managed to book a last-minute cottage at the end of July in the coastal port of Dartmouth, situated on the Devon Coastline at the mouth of the River Dart.

I'd never heard of it, but it sounded warmer than Yorkshire, and so, we went.

Dartmouth was eerily quiet for a hot summer in July. Many people were still being cautious and suspicious of anyone not adhering to the enforced rules.

The Lord kept pressing on me:

For God has not given us a spirit of fear, but of power and of love and of a sound mind. **2 Timothy 1:7**

On the first morning, I went into a deli in Dartmouth to buy a coffee, and I was told to leave because I wouldn't wear a mask. Exemptions didn't count.

The whole mask thing made me feel unwell; not that we ever need to justify things like that to anybody. Medical information is strictly confidential.

I remember that moment as a defining moment in my life, and it still makes me feel cold thinking about the hostility and segregation I faced in that place.

Oh, I nearly forgot to tell you—I am doubly blessed to have Jewish (Eastern European) ancestry on my father's side. Was this the persecution they felt buying coffee in 1930s Germany? I began to resonate.

Extraordinary behaviour.

But all of this is *so* important to the main story; you see, I knew, just like Joseph before me, that the Lord was with me, and I did not need to fear.

There would be a lesson taught, and God's goodness over my life would remain.

We went to the local church the following day. I think my family doubled the congregation, and the Vicar looked rather shocked as he walked up the aisle.

I remember the sermon was all about not living in fear.

I smiled.

We met up with him later that day at the bandstand and prayed that revival would come to Dartmouth. The spiritual warfare in that place was tangible; the kingdom of darkness rising up in the form of the occult and witchcraft, clashing against the rich Christian heritage and the faith-filled community of worshippers. The enemy definitely wasn't happy with us being there, but little did we know, this was a divine appointment—preparation time for a later date.

Later that week, we kayaked as a family up the River Dart and along the coastline to Bayard's Cove, which lies just west of the town centre. It looked interesting, and so, we then explored on foot for a closer look.

A brief history gained at Bayard's Cove, Dartmouth, Devon, England:

The background to the *Mayflower* story began when James I and his Bishops drew up a list of rules in 1604, to which all clergy were obliged to conform. However, many Anglican clergy refused, and were stripped of their positions and lost their living within the established Church of England.

William Bradford, who would later become the Governor of the Plymouth Colony in Massachusetts Bay, writes between 1630-1651:

So, the master of the bigger ship (called Mr. Jones) being consulted with, they both resolved to put into Dartmouth and have her there searched and mended, which accordingly was done, to their great charge and loss of time and fair wind. She was here thoroughly searched from stem to stern, some leaks were found and mended, and now it was conceived by the workmen and all, that she was sufficient, and they might proceed without either fear or danger.[2]

WILLIAM BRADFORD

The Bible says:

Do not fear those who kill the body but are unable to kill the soul; but rather fear Him who is able to destroy both soul and body in hell. **Matthew 10:28**

Do we have that same healthy fear of the Lord today?
Or do we choose to please and follow man instead?
Does that make life more comfortable for us?
Would speaking out for what is right mean we will have to sacrifice our jobs, our livelihoods, our pensions, our reputations?

---

[2] William Bradford, *Of Plymouth Plantation* (New York: Alfred A Knopf, 2002), 52.

Many of the Pilgrims came from villages in Nottinghamshire, Lincolnshire and Yorkshire—they received summonses for non-attendance at their local churches, and one by one they fled the country. Some settled in Leiden, in the Netherlands and lived there for some years before eventually leaving on their momentous voyage to start a colony in the United States of America.

> *Blessed are those who have been persecuted*
> *for the sake of righteousness, for theirs is the*
> *kingdom of heaven.* **Matthew 5:10**

The Bible tells us that we are to expect persecution for standing up for truth, for standing on God's Word, and for speaking out when things are not right in the culture around us—when evil is being applauded and good denounced.

> *Woe to those who call evil good, and good evil; Who*
> *substitute darkness for light and light for darkness; Who*
> *substitute bitter for sweet and sweet for bitter!* **Isaiah 5:20**

We are obliged to speak out, and the Bible says we will be blessed doing it! Christians must never be silent in the face of evil; it is our calling and our duty to speak up in the political, religious, and cultural spheres of our world when we are required to do so. Not to speak is complacency.

Will we choose to be complicit, complacent, or courageous?

I would fully endorse the reading of a book *Letter to the American Church* by author Eric Metaxas. I was randomly handed this by a friend partway through the trip and on the cover of the book it reads:

> An attenuated and unbiblical "faith," based on what
> Bonhoeffer called "cheap grace" has sapped the spiritual

vitality of millions of *Americans. Paying lip service to an insipid "evangelism," they shrink from combating the evils of our time. Metaxas refuted the pernicious lie that fighting evil politicizes Christianity. As Bonhoeffer and other heroes of the faith insisted, the Church has an irreplaceable role in the culture of a nation. It is our duty to fight the powers of darkness, especially on behalf of the weak and vulnerable.

Silence is not an option.

God calls us to defend the unborn, to confront the lies of cultural Marxism, and to battle the globalist tyranny that crushes human freedom. Confident that it is His fight, the church must overcome fear and enter the fray, armed with the spiritual weapons of prayer, self-sacrifice and love.[3]

ERIC METAXAS

*replace with a country of your choice

I was eager to discover more about these so-called Separatists and their famous voyage across the Atlantic Ocean:

The Leiden Separatists bought a small ship, the *Speedwell*, in The Netherlands. They embarked from Delftshaven on 22 July 1620, and sailed to Southampton, England to meet the *Mayflower*, which had been chartered by their English

---

[3] Eric Metaxas, *Letter to the American Church* (Washington D.C. Salem Books, 2022), cover page.

investors. There, other Separatists and additional colonists joined them.

On 15 August 1620, the *Mayflower* and *Speedwell* set sail for America. The two ships didn't get very far before the *Speedwell* began to take on water again. They changed course for **Dartmouth in Devon**, arriving on 23rd August 1620. According to the passengers the *Speedwell* was leaking like a sieve and water was penetrating her hull rapidly, causing some alarm and requiring urgent attention. Both ships lay at anchor in the harbour, **off Bayards Cove**, while repairs were carried out.

The *Mayflower* alone set sail from Plymouth, England on 16 September 1620 with just 102 passengers and crew on board. The ship arrived some 66 days later, on 11 November 1620, in Cape Cod on the US East Coast.

DARTMOUTH MAYFLOWER (2023)

I never really thought much more about the Mayflower and her intrepid voyage after that.

The remainder of that holiday was spent reading light novels on the patio, eating cream teas (the correct way round: cream first, then jam), walking the picturesque Devon coastline, and watching the little sailing boats make their effortless journeys up and down the River Dart, her waters sparkling in the mid-summer sunshine, remaining silent about those maritime stories of old.

CHAPTER THREE

*If I take up the wings of the dawn, If I dwell in the
remotest part of the sea, Even there Your hand will lead
me, And Your right hand will take hold of me.*
Psalm 139:9-10

Plymouth, Massachusetts

We touched down at Boston International Airport just after lunchtime
EST in the pouring rain.

I was still thinking about the *Jesus Revolution* movie and how much
we need a revival wave of that magnitude and impact to hit these shores
again–a tidal wave of God's presence that is so great that it would cause a
tsunami to hit the United Kingdom on the other side of the Atlantic Ocean.

Do it again, Lord.

I also knew I needed a personal detox from all the daily news and heaviness I had gladly left behind in Europe. Maybe some are yet to realise, but
we are constantly bombarded every day with bad news on the TV and radio:
propaganda, lies, and stories of a Godless worldly society that has lost its
way and openly welcomed in the antichrist spirit to take a seat at the table.

Sways of the Church of Jesus Christ has bowed down to other agendas
and consequently worshipped false gods in an attempt to keep culturally
relevant and appear kind and compassionate.

But the gospel is not about being culturally relevant in order to fit in with the particular needs and wants of that society—it's only ever about Jesus.

Will we, as Irwin W. Lutzer challenges us in his book *No Reason To Hide*, interpret the Bible through the lens of culture, or will we interpret culture through the lens of the Bible?

Jesus was and is radical.

The gospel is offensive.

Governments and authorities have also been changing legislation to suit themselves, unelected bureaucrats have been allowed to push rules and regulations, and elephants sitting in the room have been largely ignored.

As I disembarked the plane, I did wonder if America would be any better—or perhaps, would it be worse?

Either way,

Greater is He who is in me, than he who is in the world. **1 John 4:4**

The spiritual attacks started from the moment we set foot on the land.

It was clear the enemy did not want us here. If God ordains something over your life, you can be sure that Satan will do his best to destroy it.

A technical mess up concerning the hire car.

Here we go.

First, they wanted to charge us twice.

Then our luggage wouldn't fit.

Then we needed to pay an excess of $1,000 to hire another one.

Availability of cars was low. We might be stuck in Boston.

The family was getting tired, stressed, and unamused.

We waited for an hour.

Hang on, you've allowed yourself to be distracted! You're forgetting who you are and Whose you are Laura! You need to pray.

I know this stuff. It's level 1.1 of the Christian discipleship programme.

I know full well that "prayer underpins everything and is a mighty weapon in the heavenly realms, demolishing strongholds and changing our situations"—I even wrote that myself, but I haven't done it!

Dear Lord, please help us. You know all of our needs. Please send us what we need right now. In Jesus's precious name.

And there it was—like a knight in shining armour—a large white SRV came around the corner and parked right in front of us.

I swear, it had angels sitting on top and a bright light shining around it!

Thank you, God.

Faithful is He who calls you, and He also will do it. **1 Thessalonians 5:24**

The man said to us, "You can have this vehicle if you would like it?"

Who knew that Massachusetts Route 3, the highway between Bourne and Braintree, is called "Pilgrims Highway"?

Of course, it is.

I call signs like this a "God wink."

It's when the Lord speaks to you personally and intimately at that particular time in history. It doesn't matter that it might have been called that for one hundred years; it's just how that fact hits you between the eyeballs as you're driving along it.

Is that what we are God—pilgrims? People on a journey?

Pilgrim: *(noun) A person who makes a journey, often a long and difficult one, to a special place for religious reasons.*[4]

---

[4] Cambridge Dictionary (2023) *online*

Well, it hadn't been that short, and it had certainly been a challenge getting here, but I'd thought this was a family holiday before all my kids flew the nest.

We probably spent months planning this three-week vacation, where to go and what to see. Up until two days before we travelled from the UK, we were starting our USA road trip in a place called Kennebunkport up on the Maine coastline above Boston, Massachusetts.

A good friend had recommended it, and we were all set.

But something in my spirit said, "No." It was clear and loud.

So, I cancelled the trip up to Maine.

Being sensitive to the direction of the Holy Spirit in our lives is so important. As I'm typing this now, I'm smiling at another God Wink. On the notepad I used to record our adventure, there are random Bible scriptures, and for that particular day in June 2023, it was:

A man's heart plans his way, But the Lord directs his steps. **Proverbs 16:9**

You see, we can plan away (and some planning is good), but you've got to be ready and expectant for God to interrupt those plans at any given point.

Maybe He was saving us from a road traffic accident.

Or maybe it wasn't that deep.

Maybe He wanted us to go somewhere else instead.

I think He probably did.

I looked at the map to find a good place to stop for dinner between the airport and our first hotel, which was at the top of Cape Cod in a place called Buzzard's Bay.

Everywhere on that east coast has British names. Well, that makes sense.

Some of them made us laugh, like *Essex*.

I was born in a seaside town in Essex in 1979.

Plymouth looked about halfway–that sounded good, and it has a beach.

I'd like to say at that point that my mind rolled back to the summer of 2021 and it evoked memories of Bayard's Cove, Dartmouth, and the Mayflower expedition across the Atlantic Ocean–but I'm afraid it didn't.

Instead, I searched the internet for good restaurants and where to park the car.

After sixty-six days, or roughly two miserable months at sea, under the direction of Captain Christopher Jones, the ship finally reached the New World. There, the *Mayflower's* passengers found an abandoned Indian village and not much else. They also found that they were in the wrong place: Cape Cod was located at 42 degrees north latitude, well north of the Virginia Company's territory (who had given them permission to establish a settlement, or "plantation," on the East Coast between 38° and 41° North latitude)–roughly between the Chesapeake Bay (Virginia) and the mouth of the Hudson River (New York State).[5]

Technically, the Mayflower colonists had no right to be in Cape Cod at all.

In order to establish themselves as a legitimate colony at Plymouth (named after the English port from which they had departed) under these dubious circumstances, forty-one of the "Saints and Strangers" drafted and signed a document they called the Mayflower Compact (1620). This compact promised to create a "civil body politick" governed by elected officials and "just and equal laws," and it also swore allegiance to the English king.

---

[5] History.com (2023) *online*

It was the first document to establish self-government in the New World, and this early attempt at democracy set the stage for future colonists seeking independence from the British.

The colonists spent the first winter living onboard the Mayflower. Only fifty-three passengers and half the crew survived. Women were particularly hard hit; of the nineteen women who had boarded the Mayflower, only five survived the cold New England winter, confined to the ship where disease and cold were rampant. The Mayflower sailed back to England in April 1621, and once the group moved ashore, the colonists faced even more challenges.

During their first winter in America, more than half of the Plymouth colonists died from malnutrition, disease, and exposure to the harsh New England weather. In fact, without the help of the area's native people, it is likely that none of the colonists would have survived. An English-speaking Abenaki named Samoset helped the colonists form an alliance with the local Wampanoags, who taught them how to hunt local animals, gather shellfish, and grow corn, beans, and squash.

At the end of the next summer, the Plymouth colonists celebrated their first successful harvest with a three-day festival of thanksgiving.

Eventually, the Plymouth colonists were absorbed into the Puritan Massachusetts Bay Colony. Still, the Mayflower Saints and their descendants remained convinced that they alone had been specially chosen by God to act as a beacon for Christians around the world. [6]

Separatist leader William Bradford wrote this:

> As one small candle may light a thousand, so
> the light here kindled hath shone to many, yea
> in some sort to our whole nation.[7]

---

[6] History.com (2023) *online*

[7] mayflower400uk.org (2023) *online*

They called themselves "Saints"—who hoped to establish a new church in the so-called New World. Today, we often refer to the colonists who crossed the Atlantic on the Mayflower as "Pilgrims."

I have read that there are an estimated 10 million living Americans and thirty-five million people around the world who are descended from the original passengers on the Mayflower.[8]

These "Saints" in 1620 took the gospel message of the birth, death, and resurrection of Jesus Christ to the New World—I was undone.

I sat down on a bench in Pilgrim Memorial State Park, and my eyes watered.

The glory of God and the presence of the Holy Spirit took my breath away.

Looking out to sea, I could see the reconstruction of the Mayflower vessel over to the west and the remnants of Plymouth Rock encaged just behind me to the left; the statue of William Bradford standing tall further down to my right on Water Street.

How did I not know about this?

Why hadn't I joined the dots before now?

Had I been spiritually blind to what God was trying to show me?

I then remembered Dartmouth . . . and Plymouth . . . and the Pilgrim Fathers.

I wept.

If you've ever encountered the Holy Spirit in that full measure, you will know what I am speaking about. It's not something one can explain very well with just words alone.

You have to feel it.

You have to experience it.

I suddenly had an overwhelming sense of God's love for me and felt His hand upon my life. He had brought me to Plymouth, Massachusetts, and

---

[8] History.com (2023) *online*

Him alone. It was not a coincidence or something I had manufactured in my own strength. He had ordained it, and He had chosen me, us, to experience it together as a family *for such a time as this* (Esther 4:14).

I knew there had to be *more*.

I knew this was just the very beginning.

My heart leapt with a sense of excitement and awe at how great God is, and I said a prayer looking out to sea, thanking Him, praising Him, and recommitting myself to His service and to Him alone.

I managed to lose track of time and finally joined the family in a nearby restaurant. I was still feeling rather emotional, and I looked straight into my husband's eyes—he had felt it too.

No words were necessary.

He had also been up to the statue and looked at the two inscriptions. I'll never forget reading these words for the first time from a photograph on his iPhone:

> *So they left ye goodly & pleasante citie, which had been their resting place nere 12 years, but they knew they were pilgrimes & looked not much on those things, but lift up their eyes to ye Heavens, their dearest cuntrie and quieted their spirits.* **William Bradford**

A timely reminder that as Christians, *we are not citizens of earth, but of Heaven* (Philippians 3:20), *that we set our minds on things above, not on earthly things* (Colossians 3:2). That we are pilgrims – called by God to *heal the sick, raise the dead, cleanse those with leprosy, cast out demons* (Matthew 10:8) and to *go and make disciples of all nations, baptizing them in the name of the Father and the Son and the Holy Spirit, teaching them to observe all that Jesus has commanded us, and that He will be with us always, even to the end of the age* (Matthew 28:19-20).

Lastly (and which was not least) a great hope and inward zeal they had of laying some good foundation (or at least to make some way therunto) for ye propagating & advancing ye Gospell of ye Kingdom of Christ in those remote parts of ye world, yea, though they should be but even as stepping stones unto others for ye performing of so a great work.
William Bradford

The Mayflower Saints were the first evangelists to the United States of America, and here I was, in this moment, over 400 years later, as a carrier of the same gospel message of salvation, hope, love, and transformation.

And these Pilgrims before me have laid the very *stepping stones* for me to come and allow me to do such things. As the Psalmist writes, *"Such knowledge is too wonderful for me; it is too high, I cannot comprehend it"* (Psalm 139).

I was undone all over again.

CHAPTER FOUR

Our willingness to be used as God's vessels can make
His father-heart a reality to our hurting world.
Floyd McClung[9]

Southend-on-Sea, Essex

We're all on a spiritual journey, but where did *my* spiritual journey begin?

Because we all have a story. You have a story too—and if you've made it to this point in the book, I'm so grateful for you.

Well, this is my story.

To begin with, I need to take you right back to the spring of 1954 in North-West London. Frank, probably the most wonderful man I've ever met and a first-class athlete in his prime, was signed for Brentford Football Club. A chance conversation with a fellow teammate in the dressing room after the match led to an unplanned evening visit to the Haringey Arena to see Billy Graham, and my grandfather, Frank, was saved.

He had an encounter with the Living God for the first time in his life, and he was never the same again.

I do often wonder who that teammate was—because I would like to thank him.

---

[9] Floyd McClung, Father Heart of God (2004)

That domino of events then meant my grandfather took my mother to church from a young age, and then she, in turn, took my siblings and me, and so, being part of a church community was a normality for me growing up.

But at the age of around twelve, it had become largely irrelevant.

A sleepy, cold, somewhat boring Church of England (Anglican) service was simply not doing it, and had it not been that my mother thought to move us to the all-singing, all-dancing, lively Baptist congregation up the road, then I fear my faith experience would have been lost completely at that point.

There are many reasons people go to church, and I'm not ashamed to say that for me, at the age of thirteen, it was the drummer who caught my eye.

I then discovered access to an enormous, vibrant youth group; something that the previous parish church was sadly lacking. There was never a dull moment; there was always somewhere to go, always someone to speak to. Each week, from Sunday to Saturday, was filled with activities and opportunities. I totally loved it, and I'm forever thankful for my youth leaders, who I know invested so much of their time and resources into myself and others.

But I didn't really know Jesus.

We talked about Him, read about Him, and sang about Him—but who was He, and why did He come to be with us on Earth?

In September of 1992, I went along to a Christian rally in my local town, probably not too dissimilar to that which my grandfather had experienced in Haringey forty years prior. There was a visiting American evangelist speaking named Floyd McClung, and I remember being totally fascinated by this man because he'd given up his comfortable life in the United States of America and moved with his wife and young children to live and work in the notorious and dangerous Red Light District of Amsterdam, where he pioneered an urban base for an organisation called YWAM (Youth With a Mission).

That story just blew my mind when I heard it!

And that evening was the first time I encountered the power of the Holy Spirit for myself. Up until that point, it had been all head knowledge. And at that moment, I allowed it to move into my heart.

You see, people can tell you about God; they can describe to you who Jesus is and try and prove His existence with historical landmarks and shared testimonies—but when you *encounter* the presence of God through the *power* of the Holy Spirit, it changes everything.

At the end of the Book of Luke, which is one of the Gospel accounts of the New Testament, Jesus says to His disciples:

> *And behold, I am sending the promise of My Father*
> *upon you; but you are to stay in the city* **until you**
> **are clothed with power from on high**.
> **Luke 24:49**

That clothing He is talking about is the gift of the Holy Spirit—the priceless deposit Jesus left for us on Earth after His resurrection and before the ascension up to Heaven to be with the Father.

The meeting was held in a big round white Circus-like tent, and I remember being projected out of my tiered seating at the back where I was sat with a group of friends and literally catapulted to the front of the stage where I met with the speaker and gave my life to Jesus.

In another of the Gospels (John), Jesus describes the Holy Spirit as the "Helper"—a powerful force that continues to teach us, guide us, and strengthen us in the absence of the physical person of Jesus here on Earth. The same Spirit which has been living and moving amongst all people for 2,000 years, the same power which rose Jesus from the dead, and the same power which pushed me out of my seat thirty years ago and moved me to the front of the auditorium to make the most important decision of my life, is here with me, with you, right now.

So, I had experienced a huge spiritual encounter, aged just thirteen. I believed that God was real—but why Jesus?

I think that's what Jesus meant when He said:

> *Allow the children to come to Me; do not forbid them, for the kingdom of God belongs to such as these. Truly I say to you, whoever does not receive the kingdom of God like a child will not enter it at all.* **Mark 10:13-16**

I believed because I felt it and experienced it—not because I understood everything. I think, as adults, we need the answers about something first before we can fully trust anything—and that's often a good practise.

There's a lot of deception, confusion, and lies in the world, and the gift of discernment and knowledge is of utmost importance.

But when it comes to faith, just like the whole of the kingdom of God, it's all upside down. After the resurrection Jesus said to His doubting disciple Thomas, who insisted seeing the holes in His hands where the nails had been driven and the large open wound in His side before he would believe that Jesus had really risen from the dead:

> *Because you have seen Me, have you believed? Blessed are they who did not see, and yet believed.* **John 20:29**

Because, after all, that's simply what faith is—it's trust.
Martin Luther King Jr. said:

> *Faith is taking the first step even when you don't see the whole staircase.*[10]

---

[10] Martin Luther King Jr., *"Speech to commemorate the centennial of the Preliminary Emancipation Proclamation"*, Park Sheraton Hotel, New York City (September 12th, 1962)

Every time you sit down in a chair, you are exercising faith.

The apostle Paul, formally an evil persecutor and barbaric killer of Christians who met Jesus in a profound spiritual experience on the Road to Damascus, became probably the best evangelist who ever lived, said this about the Christian life:

We walk by faith, not by sight. **2 Corinthians 5:7**

You see, faith in God would not be "faith" if we had all the answers and knew everything about everything—only God knows that.

When Floyd McClung preached in that tent in Southend-on-Sea in September 1992, my heart was broken for the affliction of all God's people, and I understood then, as I believe now, that it is only the life-transforming power of the gospel of Jesus Christ that could and will, without doubt, set them free.

I knew I was being called as an evangelist then, and various encounters with God since have confirmed and affirmed that commissioning.

I wouldn't call myself a saint, or even a pilgrim for that matter, but I definitely want the whole world to know that *Jesus saves.*

CHAPTER FIVE

*Give me one hundred preachers who fear nothing but sin, and
desire nothing but God, and I care not a straw whether they
be clergymen or laymen; such alone will shake the gates
of hell and set up the kingdom of heaven on Earth.*
John Wesley[11]

Martha's Vineyard, Massachusetts

We set off early the next day from Buzzard's Bay to catch the early
morning ferry from Woods Hole on the mainland to Oak Bluffs on
Martha's Vineyard.

As unaware as I was about the history of Plymouth just twenty-four
hours previously, I was equally blinded to what was about to be revealed here.

The local Chamber of Commerce describes Martha's Vineyard as a
*"picturesque island paradise, just 7 miles off the coast of Massachusetts but a
world away from the hustle and bustle of the mainland."*

That sounded good enough to me.

I'd heard of it in a trivial sense—I knew that some of the American poli-
ticians and diplomats owned real estate there and that it was the setting for
some iconic movies such as *Jaws* and *The Ghostwriter*, but that was about it.

---

[11] John Wesley, Good Reads *online*

A prophetic friend had prayed for me a few days before leaving the UK, saying that something significant would be revealed on this trip and to go expectant—something would *mark* me, and it would change me, and I would have no doubt that I had seen Him. After which, he said, I would have no doubt in my mind to boldly declare:

"I have seen the Lord."

As I sat on the top deck of the ferry, looking forward toward the island with the warm sea breeze blowing onto my face, I pondered for a moment if this was to happen on Martha's Vineyard.

It was cloudy first thing, and a deep mist had set over the sea, making it difficult to make out the contours of the land and where we were heading.

Sometimes life can be like that.

We know where we need to be heading—we have a clear destination in our minds—but we can't see more than a few metres ahead of us.

I was slightly disappointed not to have a clear view from the top deck and said a prayer for a safe and easy passage across.

Our boat arrived at Oak Bluffs, a small, picturesque harbour town on the eastern shores of Martha's Vineyard at around 11 a.m. in the morning.

We had a typical leisure day planned of cycling and exploring the island on foot, swimming in the sea (avoiding the sharks), eating legendary ice creams, and visiting quaint Edgartown, a former whaling port with an interesting history and a chance to do a spot of shopping.

We took a short pause at midpoint, and I stood for a while on the famous "Jaws Bridge" looking across Cow Bay toward the horizon of the Atlantic Ocean.

The words of Mayor Vaughan in the movie echoed through my head:

As you see, it's a beautiful day. The beaches are open, and people are having a wonderful time.[12]

The fictitious "Amity Island" (set on Martha's Vineyard) was completely dependent on the economic boost during the summer months, and if the beaches were closed, the tourists would have taken their business elsewhere.

Whilst the killer fish still lurked in the waters beneath, the deadly shark attack had to be covered up by the authorities at all lengths to avoid financial ruin.

Oh, the irony.

As I cycled along Beach Road, the popular six-mile designated bicycle path between Oak Bluffs and Edgartown, I first became aware of the spiritual warfare in that place. It was intense and overwhelming.

A place of political, lifestyle, and occultic strongholds—a battle for control and territory. A battle between the kingdom of light and the kingdom of darkness.

As I walked the streets of Edgartown, passing the beautiful wooden colonial-style housing and quaint shops and churches, I prayed in the spirit (that means to pray in *tongues*, a heavenly language, and, for me, in English – as the Holy Spirit leads) a warfare prayer against the powers and principalities that were colliding in the heavenly realms, and I asked God to break in, expose the evil and deception, and flood His light and His truth back into the place.

On the way back to our bikes after lunch, I recall my husband and I exchanged unusual cross words over something trivial that had once more blown up into disproportion. We both knew that the high energy supernatural atmosphere was messing with our heads and our spirits, but we had let it affect us.

This was quickly resolved. We forgave one another, and we moved on.

---

[12] Steven Spielberg, John Williams. *JAWS*. USA, 1975

But I could sense how the enemy had gained a foothold on this island, how demonic doors had been opened and how that would impact the spiritual atmosphere my husband and I were both feeling—but I was then intrigued to find out the island's spiritual history and Christian influence. That took me back to Oak Bluffs and Wesleyan Grove.

Wesleyan Grove is a 34-acre (14 ha) National Historic Landmark District in Oak Bluffs. It was named in honour of the great revivalist John Wesley, the founder of the Methodist Church. Formally known as the *Martha's Vineyard Campmeeting Association (MVCMA)* or the *Campgrounds*, it was the first summer religious camp established in the United States. It is famous for its approximately 300 colourful houses in a style now described as Carpenter Gothic—ornate, gingerbread cottages were built in an oak grove around a central church tabernacle.

From the first camp meeting in 1835 until 1859, ministers preached from a crudely constructed stand. In 1859, Perez Mason built a larger and more aesthetically pleasing preachers' stand. It was large enough to seat 30, and it included lattice screen supports, movable rear shutters for ventilation, and a roof that was angled to amplify the voice of the speaker. Seating for congregations of up to 4,000 was constructed during that period. In 1869, a huge tent was raised over Wesleyan Grove to protect the congregation from the heat and the rain. The tent was used each season until the erection of the current open-air iron Tabernacle in 1879. It was built by John W. Hoyt of Springfield, Massachusetts and has seating for over 2,000

It was the physical and spiritual centre of the Campground.

Just after the American Civil War, the area developed as a large Methodist summer campground with open air Christian revival meetings. This meeting style became popular around the United States at the time, and many other similar camps were founded using similar models.

The first so-called campmeeting in what became known as Wesleyan Grove was held in 1835. Over subsequent years, participants began arriving early and staying after the revival. Nine tents provided shelter for the first campers in 1835, but as the campers grew in number, families chose to pitch tents of their own; there were 100 tents in 1851 and that increased to 320 by 1858, located around the preaching ground. During one Sunday in summer 1858, there were a full 20,000 people listening to a sermon.

It was in the 1860s and 1870s, that the family tents were rapidly replaced with the permanent wooden cottages.

In subsequent years the congregations grew enormously, and many of the thousands in attendance were housed in large tents known as "society tents." A congregation from a church on the mainland would maintain its own society tent. Between 1855 and 1865 the campmeetings began to change in character. They continued to be religious in nature, but the participants also began to enjoy the benefit of the sea air and social interaction as they revived both mind and body.

Many eminent members of the clergy from across the country have preached at the campmeetings in Wesleyan Grove. That tradition continues today, although services are no longer held day and night as they were in the early years. Over time, the Martha's Vineyard Camp Meeting Association has become increasingly interdenominational, and the current members of the Board of Directors are affiliated with a wide variety of religious groups. The religious services and special programs of the Association all have a strong ecumenical spirit[13].

It was fascinating to discover that this little island on the eastern coast of the United States of America had been the home of big revival meetings.

The spiritual energy was tangible.

I noted that Wesleyan Grove was named after John Wesley (b. 1703), the Anglican English clergyman, evangelist, and brother of Charles who, together, founded the Methodist movement in England.

In that moment, I remembered "Wesley's Tree" in Winchelsea, Cheshire—a place where John had preached his final open-air sermon in 1790 and called the inhabitants of the town to *repent and believe in the Gospel, for the Kingdom of God is at hand.*" (Mark 1:15). Four years prior, I had stood under that tree with a good friend; we'd buried scriptures and made a covenant with the Lord that we would carry on the work of Wesley and be evangelists to the nations.

John Wesley, the second son of Samuel, was a former nonconformist and dissenter from the Church of England.

I was beginning to see a pattern.

Wesley viewed his mission in life as one of proclaiming the good news of salvation by faith, which he did whenever a

---

13 Wikipedia online, *Wesleyan Grove* (2023)

pulpit was offered him. The congregations of the Church of England, however, soon closed their doors to him because of his enthusiasm. He then went to religious societies, trying to inject new spiritual vigour into them instead.

For a year he worked through existing church societies, but resistance to his methods increased. In 1739, George Whitfield, who later became an important preacher of the Great Awakening in Great Britain and North America, persuaded Wesley to go to the unchurched masses.

Many of Wesley's preachers had gone to the American Colonies, but after the American Revolution most returned to England. Because the Bishop of London would not ordain some of his preachers to serve in the United States, Wesley controversially took it upon himself, in 1784, to do so.

In the same year he pointed out that his societies operated independently of any control by the Church of England.[14]

The religious institutions closed the doors on him because of his enthusiasm.
Sounds familiar.
George Whitfield persuaded Wesley to go to the unchurched masses.
A man after my own heart.
He was prevented by the Bishop of London from preaching in the United States, but he went anyway.
Sounds to me that Wesley had a healthy fear of the Lord and not a fear of man.

---

[14] Wikipedia online, *Wesleyan Grove* (2023)

Well done good and faithful servant. **Matthew 25:23**

From a handful of spiritually seeking people in 1835 to 20,000 worshippers in 1858, the camp meetings on Martha's Vineyard continued to grow in number and power, and many people came to faith in Jesus Christ.

You will know them by their fruits. Grapes are not gathered
from thorn bushes, nor figs from thistles, are they? So
every good tree bears good fruit, but the bad tree bears
bad fruit. A good tree cannot bear bad fruit, nor can a
bad tree bear good fruit. Every tree that does not bear
good fruit is cut down and thrown into the fire. So then,
you will know them by their fruits. **Matthew 7:16-20**

This fruit made me hungry for revival and thirsty for more of God.
William Bradford, a Pilgrim and Saint. John Wesley, a theologian and clergyman. Lonnie Frisbee, a Pentecostal hippie.
God's evangelists come in all shapes and sizes, and the Lord uses us all.

Then I heard the voice of the Lord saying, "Whom
shall I send? And who will go for us?" And I
said, "Here am I. Send me!" **Isaiah 6:8**

I later discovered that the English explorer Bartholomew Gosmold discovered wild grapes growing on the island in 1602, but I do wonder whether there is a more prophetic meaning to Martha's Vineyard?
One thing remains—the harvest is plentiful.
And we need more workers in the landowner's vineyard.

CHAPTER SIX

When you pass through the waters, I will be with you; And through the rivers, they will not overflow you. When you walk through the fire, you will not be scorched, Nor will the flame burn you.

Isaiah 43:2

Chatham, Massachusetts

Back on the mainland, we had two free days in our schedule to explore the beauty and magnificence of Cape Cod.

First stop, Chatham.

Encompassing a mere 16 square miles of high ground and surrounded on three sides by water, Chatham has a beauty that is unsurpassed. The town is a decidedly maritime place of pristine beaches, wild barrier islands, tidal shoals, fleeting sandbars, circular coves and miles of saltwater inlets.

Incorporated in 1712, Chatham remains remarkably old-fashioned, despite a well-deserved reputation for shopping. Chic boutiques reside in quaint storefronts along its winding

Main Street lined with historic inns, white-steepled churches, trendy eateries and art galleries.[15]

Awesome. I think we may have something for everyone here—and when you're a family of five ranging from sixteen to forty-six years of age, both male and female, trust me, that's of high importance.

On the afternoon of 9th November, 1620, the *Mayflower* came to a turning point in the dangerous Pollack Rip off Chatham. There, Captain Christopher Jones steered the ship north, effectively ending its voyage to the Hudson River. Two days later the ship anchored in Provincetown where it remained for roughly five weeks before sailing west to Plymouth.

Chatham profoundly shaped Pilgrim history because of its dangerous waters offshore. Had the Mayflower been able to continue to the Hudson River area, there would be no Cape Cod, Plymouth or New England Pilgrim story. Nor would there have been a Mayflower Compact, the first self-governing document written in the New World.[16]

Reading the plaque located on Main Street at the parking area of the Chatham Lighthouse Beach Overlook, it reminded me of the movie *Sliding*

---

[15] Nickerson Family Association (2023) *Chatham, The Turning Point: The Mayflower and the Nickersons*

[16] Nickerson Family Association (2023) *Chatham, The Turning Point: The Mayflower and the Nickersons*

Doors—if you missed that one, it's a classic 1990s film starring actress Gwyneth Paltrow.

The movie alternates between two storylines, showing two separate paths the central character's life could take depending on whether (or not) she catches a certain underground train.

Had the Mayflower been able to continue to the Hudson River area, there would be no Cape Cod, Plymouth or New England Pilgrim story.

Sometimes, the consequences of our direct actions of free will lead to a change in the direction of our lives, and sometimes, God will intervene or interject, and we no longer have control of where our life is going.

There is much more I'd like to say on that a little later in the book.

It's important in the latter scenario that we humble ourselves and submit to *"His good, pleasing, and perfect will"* (Romans 12:2) and know that the eternal God has determined the absolute best plan to carry out His will for us.

And we know that God causes all things to work together for good to those who love God, to those who are called according to His purpose. **Romans 8:28**

I suspect the Pilgrims on the Mayflower had no choice about the matter; the waters on the eastern seaboard were treacherous, and so rather than heading for the Hudson River, they continued their exhausting voyage northward toward Provincetown and finally, settled in Plymouth.

The Psalmist writes:

Your eyes have seen my formless substance; And in Your book were written All the days that were ordained for me, When as yet there was not one of them. **Psalm 139:16**

God is omnipresent and omniscient—He is everywhere and in everything.

His "universal presence", which is everywhere and in everything all at the same time, and His "limitless power" to do whatever He chooses.

The Lord knows every little detail about us, and the Bible tells us that He has numbered our days; He ordains when we shall live and when we will die.

The real question is: How will we, or how should we, respond?

Well, the Lord Jesus Himself said it like this:

> *"Pray, then, in this way: 'Our Father who is in heaven, Hallowed be Your name. Your kingdom come. **Your will be done, On earth as it is in heaven**. Give us this day our daily bread. And forgive us our debts, as we also have forgiven our debtors. And do not lead us into temptation, but deliver us from evil.'"* **Matthew 6:9-13**

Let *your* will be done, Lord.

Those lazy and peaceful days on Cape Cod which followed gave me the gift of some time and space to process the significant events, markers, and signposts that the Lord, in His infinite grace, was revealing to me step by step on this trip.

It was becoming more and more apparent that we did not plan this itinerary but that the Lord had gone before us and planned it all.

Nothing was a coincidence.

We visited the delightful and vibrant towns of Dennis, Yarmouth, and Hyannis—the historic childhood home of former United States President John F. Kennedy.

We ate the best fish tacos at Harwich Port.

We laid out on the beach at Chapin Memorial and watched the sand dunes disappear.

We sat by the campfire and stood in awe at the sunset over Lewis Bay. All was well in the world, and my soul was at rest.

CHAPTER SEVEN

If freedom is to survive and prosper, it will require the sacrifice, the effort and the thoughtful attention of every citizen.
John F. Kennedy[17]

Newport, Rhode Island

The following morning, we drove the stunning eighty-mile journey across the waterways from Yarmouth, Cape Cod, to Newport in Rhode Island.

It had been recommended to us as an interesting port of call on route to Long Island, New York, via Connecticut, and it made sense to break up the journey and enjoy visiting another state along the East Coast.

Our family has always enjoyed walking and trekking, and I had discovered the three-and-a-half-mile famous cliff walk along the Newport shoreline, which includes the rich architectural history of the town's gilded age, wildflowers, birds, and geology.

> The Puritan British theologian Roger Williams (1603–1683) is often given the sole role of founder of Rhode Island, however, the colony was in fact settled by five independent and combative sets of people between 1636 and 1642.

---

[17] John F. Kennedy, Good Reads *online*

They were all English, and most of them began their colonial experiences in Massachusetts Bay colony but were banished for various reasons. Roger Williams' group was the earliest: In 1636, he settled in what would become Providence on the north end of Narragansett Bay, after he was kicked out of the Massachusetts Bay colony.

Roger Williams had grown up in England, only leaving in 1630 with his wife Mary Barnard when the persecution of Puritans and Separatists began increasing. He moved to the Massachusetts Bay Colony and worked from 1631 to 1635 as a pastor and a farmer.

Although many in the colony saw his views as quite radical, Williams felt that the religion he practiced must be free from any influence of the Church of England and the English King. In addition, he questioned the right of the King to grant land to individuals in the New World.

While serving as a pastor in Salem, he had a fight with the colonial leaders because he believed that each church congregation should be autonomous and should not follow directions sent down from the leaders.

In 1635, Williams was banished back to England by the Massachusetts Bay Colony for his beliefs in the separation of church and state and freedom of religion.[18]

---

[18] ThoughtCo. (2023) *How Rhode Island Colony Was Founded.*

Roger Williams was yet another English theologian who was forced to emigrate to the United States of America to avoid the increasing persecution of Puritans and Separatists by the Church of England.

This revelation prompted me to dig a little deeper.

I wanted to know why the Puritans and Separatists were being persecuted in the first place.

I told you—I like to ask questions.

> Puritanism was a religious reform movement in the late 16th and 17th centuries that sought to "purify" the Church of England of remnants of the Roman Catholic "popery" that the Puritans claimed had been retained after the religious settlement reached early in the reign of Queen Elizabeth I. Puritans became noted in the 17th century for a spirit of moral and religious earnestness that informed their whole way of life, and they sought through church reform to make their lifestyle the pattern for the whole nation. Their efforts to transform the nation contributed both to civil war in England and to the founding of colonies in America as working models of the Puritan way of life.[19]

Although they had much in common, Puritans and Separatists were also distinctly different.

> While the Separatists believed that the only way to live according to Biblical precepts was to leave the Church of England entirely, the Puritans thought they could reform the church from within. Sometimes called *non-separating Puritans*, this less radical group shared a lot in common

---

[19] ThoughtCo. (2023) *How Rhode Island Colony Was Founded.*

with the Separatists, particularly a form of worship and self-organization called "the congregational way."

The biggest difference between the Separatists and the Puritans was that the Puritans believed they could live out the congregational way in their local churches without abandoning the larger Church of England.

The Puritans, however, were content to have an ecclesiastical structure above them, but they sought to operate as a congregation in a biblical way; on the other hand, the Separatists felt that they needed to completely separate themselves and have their congregational community separate from the state church.[20]

Reading all of this, I am challenged to consider: Is this really any different to how one might feel today about false doctrine being preached and ungodly agendas and practices being celebrated in the Church?

The British Encyclopaedia states that the Puritans had a "spirit of moral and religious earnestness that informed their whole way of life."[21]

The religious spirit is a type of demonic spirit that influences a person or group of people to replace a genuine relationship with God with works and traditions to earn their own salvation. It has established nonbiblical beliefs and customs for generations, and it has crept into many churches (and other faiths) with a purpose to cause judgment and destruction among the body of believers.

---

[20] ThoughtCo. (2023) *How Rhode Island Colony Was Founded.*

[21] Encyclopaedia Britannica (2023) *online*

Of course, this all rather depends on your definition of *religious*.

When somebody says to me, "Laura, you're *religious*, aren't you?" I cringe.

I'm a woman of deep faith and a follower of the Lord Jesus Christ; religion is a manmade concept, which I do my best to avoid.

For anybody reading this book and on the discovery stages of a spiritual pilgrimage, I'm sorry if this sounds like an oxymoron to you—it isn't.

And I think whoever wrote that paragraph about *religious earnestness* in the Britannica Encyclopaedia probably misunderstood its real meaning!

It seems to me as though the Puritans had a *biblical earnestness* and an *orthodox standing point*.

We seem to live in a world now where up is down and left is right.

There is no moral compass anymore because the largely secularised world has abandoned the faith in the one true God of the Bible (Yahweh) and aligned itself with an antichrist, satanic agenda. This means it celebrates, honours, and applauds that which is in direct rebellion to God and His ways.

God (and the Bible) upholds the traditional family unit: the sanctification of marriage between one man and one woman for life, the care of the unborn, two genders, male and female, made in His image, and humankind as the pinnacle of His creation.

We are constantly being bombarded by the mainstream media, governments, education systems, social media, and sadly, some misled and apostate churches, to put aside our deep-held, conservative Christian beliefs and, instead, accept their secular and liberal worldviews. This growing cultural shift includes ideologies such as transgenderism, artificial intelligence, virtual reality, transhumanism, LGBTQ, critical race theory, abortion, and the climate change agenda.

Does that make me a Puritan or a Separatist? Or do I have a *moral and religious earnestness* because I simply believe in the precepts of God's Holy Word and commandments and seek to uphold godly values and standards within a morally bankrupt society?

As I type this, the Church of England is in disarray over sexuality issues, and we could be on the precipice of another separatist movement on this side of the pond. For my American family, I know you have been here before.

It was decided in February 2023 that Church of England priests will be permitted to bless the civil marriages of same-sex couples in a profound shift in the Church's stance on homosexuality after a historic vote by its governing body at General Synod in London.

The media reported there was an immediate backlash from the Global South Fellowship of Anglican Churches (GSFA), which represents churches in twenty-four countries and provinces, including Nigeria, Kenya, Uganda and Rwanda, who said the Church of England's new stance on the doctrine of marriage was against the overwhelming mind of the Anglican Communion.[22]

Not only that, but the state church in England (the head of the Church of England is King Charles III) has also aligned itself with immoral, illegal, illiberal, and unethical governmental dictates and ungodly and worldly agendas.

It has clearly forgotten it is under the directive of the Magna Carta—the religious freedom of the Church, and her liberty to worship at all times.

The Magna Carta 1297 is still celebrated as the foundation stone of English democracy and rule of law. It's very first chapter reads -

"FIRST, We have granted to God, and by this our present Charter have confirmed, for Us and our Heirs for ever, that the Church of England shall be free, and shall have all her whole Rights and Liberties inviolable."

---

[22] The Guardian, *Anglicans reject Justin Welby as head of global church amid anger at same-sex blessings*, 20th February 2023

Most of the other provisions of Magna Carta have been repealed by now; but not this one.[23]

- ❖ Churches should never have closed during lockdown.
- ❖ Churches should not have opened up as vaccination centres.
- ❖ Holy Scripture should not have been abused to make people comply.
- ❖ The leaders of the Church should not have been political.
- ❖ Congregants should not have been separated due to a medical choice.
- ❖ Priests and pastors should not have been cautioned, fined, or arrested for giving pastoral care to their parishioners and opening their churches for worship.

In the United Kingdom, many people during that time tried to fight back with a form of civil disobedience, but the reality is that they were made to feel intimidated, unclean, unwanted, and under persecution.

I was one of those people.

Has the state church apologised or learned from its unlawful actions? Not yet.

Is there hope that it will?

There is always hope.

We went for a long, family walk along the coastal path, passing the Vanderbilt Mansion, the Salve Regina University, and up Ruggles Avenue.

I sat quietly by myself and watched the giant Atlantic waves crashing against the jagged rocks and processed and prayed much about the trauma and tribulation I have spoken about and that many of us have been through.

The noise of the ocean and the majesty of creation moved my spirit once more.

---

[23] Christian Concern (2023) *Magna Carta and Church Freedom in a World of Lockdown*

For I am the Lord your God, who stirs up the sea so that its waves roar (the Lord of armies is His name). **Isaiah 51:15**

It was a timely reminder that God is Sovereign and He is above all powers and principalities.

Even the wind and the waves obey him. **Matthew 8:27**

We must not live in fear.

Stay free.

Later that evening, we took a gentle stroll around Newport and stumbled unexpectedly upon St. Mary's Roman Catholic Church–the church which celebrated the marriage of John F. Kennedy to Jacqueline Bouvier on September 12, 1953.

I recalled the recording of President John F. Kennedy's remarks on March 6, 1962, concerning President Franklin D. Roosevelt's 1941 State of the Union Address (also known as the "Four Freedoms" speech), during which President Roosevelt identified four fundamental freedoms that everyone ought to enjoy.

These included freedom of speech, freedom of worship, freedom from want, and freedom from fear.[24]

I have closely followed his nephew Robert F. Kennedy Jr, the environmental lawyer, campaigner for public health, and founder of Children's Health Defense.

As I type, he is also running to be president of the USA in the next election.

I smiled at the irony of it all, but it felt like another *God Wink.*

---

[24] President John F. Kennedy, March 6th 1962

It's devastating to think that only eighteen months after that iconic speech about freedom, John F. Kennedy was assassinated.

CHAPTER EIGHT

Darkness cannot drive out darkness; only light can do that.
Hate cannot drive out hate; only love can do that.
Martin Luther King, Jr.[25]

Long Beach, New York

Today was a big drive day by British standards.

We travelled four hours and just short of two hundred miles of American interstate.

And not to mention, this included five differing opinions of what music to listen to in the car, when to stop for coffee, and where best to fill up the tank with gas.

Our first choice for coffee was a big mistake. It was not a nice neighbourhood!

Discernment.

OK, I think I'll keep driving!

Coffee can wait guys.

On the way to Long Beach, we stopped off at a small town called Oyster Bay, located at the top of the island but still in Nassau County. In 1995, as an excited teenager, I spent about ten days there visiting friends of my parents and hadn't had the opportunity to go back and visit.

Almost thirty years later, it was a joy and a privilege to stand on the same beach and walk up familiar streets, locate properties of meaning—the house, the church, the Italian deli, the laundrette—reminisce about what had been as a teenager, but also to give thanks to Him for the life I lead now and the hilltops and valleys I have passed though in-between.

And then to come back with my own family all those years later, to re-live that history and make brand new memories with them, was a total joy for me.

Life is so fast-paced these days, and people have a tendency to want to be busy, to fill their lives up with so many things—material things and activities—that somehow, they won't then have to stop, think, and reflect.

The Lord commands us to stop from time to time—to take Sabbath, to take a pit-stop rest.

It's a biblical principle, and He made us that way.

It's healing for our body, our mind, our spirit, and our soul.

And for that brief moment on the beach at Oyster Bay Cove, I did just that. I intentionally pulled myself away from the hustle and the bustle, from the questions and the planning, from the noise and distraction, and I simply spent some time with God and thanked Him.

It wasn't a long time. Perhaps only fifteen minutes.

Jesus says in the Gospels:

> *Come to Me, all who are weary and burdened, and I will give you rest. Take My yoke upon you and learn from Me, for I am gentle and humble in heart, and you will find rest for your souls. For My yoke is comfortable, and My burden is light.* **Matthew 11:28-30**

Long Beach became a city in 1922 and is one of the older, more established communities on Long Island. Founded in 1880 when the first Long Beach Hotel was built, it continued to grow at a steady pace (the Long Island railroad arrived in 1882 promoting Long Beach as a resort community for vacationers).

With the ocean on one side and the bay on the other, Long Beach developed as a seaside community. By the beach on the oceanfront there is a 2 ¼ mile long boardwalk (built in 1914 with the help of some elephants). A section of the boardwalk is set aside as a bicycle lane and the recent interest in physical fitness has resulted in an increased use of the lighted boardwalk both during the day and at night. The adjacent beach is a 3.5 mile stretch of pure white sand open to the public year-round.[26]

I've enjoyed running outdoors for about twelve years.

It's notoriously been my quiet time to listen to God, to pray, and to worship.

I've never been very good at keeping still, and some people find it hard to understand how running can equate to stillness and peace and a closeness to Jesus—but for me, it works.

As the Scottish athlete Eric Liddell said after he won the gold medal in the 1924 Paris Olympics, "*God made me for a purpose. God made me fast and when I run, I feel His pleasure.*"[27]

---

[26] Long Beach New York. (2023) *Long Beach New York—The City by the Sea.*

[27] Eric Liddell, Good Reads *online*

I can't say He made me particularly fast, but I certainly feel His pleasure when I run.

And so, whenever I travel, being able to run is an important factor to keep me mentally focussed, spiritually grounded and physically in shape.

The two-and-a-quarter-mile long boardwalk at Long Beach was a welcome surprise, and I planned to wake up early before the sun got too hot and run the entire length there and back from our hotel the following morning.

The Lord spoke to me a lot that evening about spiritual warfare—what the Bible talks about as "the rising up" between the kingdom of God and the kingdom of darkness (Matthew 24:7). The last few years in particular have felt like a perpetual battle for us as a family—physically and spiritually— and it is a concept that many new believers and those who are exploring and questioning the Christian faith have frequently reported to me.

I remember speaking to one woman over social media in the height of the national lockdowns and sharing my own faith journey. She said this to me:

Laura, I never realised that God existed until I was faced with the presence of pure evil.

As an evangelist, I love how new believers see things so simply and so clearly.

As Christians, we are to put on daily the armour of God and pray protection over our lives and our families.

Finally, be strong in the Lord and in the strength of His might. Put on the full armour of God, so that you will be able to stand firm against the schemes of the devil. For our struggle is not against flesh and blood, but against the rulers, against the powers, against the world forces of this darkness, against the spiritual forces of wickedness in the heavenly places.

*Therefore, take up the full armour of God, so that you
will be able to resist on the evil day, and having done
everything, to stand firm. Stand firm therefore, having
belted your waist with truth, and having put on the
breastplate of righteousness, and having strapped on your
feet the preparation of the gospel of peace; in addition
to all, taking up the shield of faith with which you will be
able to extinguish all the flaming arrows of the evil one.*

*And take the helmet of salvation and the sword of the
Spirit, which is the word of God.* **Ephesians 6:10-17**

The Bible tells us straight that the *"thief [Satan] comes to steal, kill and destroy"* (John 10:10) and that he *"prowls around like a roaring lion, seeking someone to devour"* (1 Peter 5:8).

He particularly goes after Christians who are new to the faith and those who are active and equipped doing transformational kingdom work, preaching the gospel, healing the sick, and setting people free in the name of Jesus.

My husband and I lead a local ministry, and we feel commissioned by God to speak truth, often being on the frontline and at the cutting edge of healing, deliverance, and salvation. It's important to armour up and pray a hedge of angelic protection and for God to lead us in everything we do.

Psalm 91 is another scripture which has sustained us on many an occasion:

*One who dwells in the shelter of the Most High
Will lodge in the shadow of the Almighty.
I will say to the Lord, "My refuge and my fortress,
My God, in whom I trust!"
For it is He who rescues you from the net of the trapper*

And from the deadly plague.
He will cover you with His pinions,
And under His wings you may take refuge;
His faithfulness is a shield and wall.
You will not be afraid of the terror by night,
Or of the arrow that flies by day;
Of the plague that stalks in darkness,
Or of the destruction that devastates at noon.

A thousand may fall at your side
And ten thousand at your right hand,
But it shall not approach you.
You will only look on with your eyes
And see the retaliation against the wicked.

For you have made the Lord, my refuge,
The Most High, your dwelling place.
No evil will happen to you,
Nor will any plague come near your tent.
For He will give His angels orders concerning you,
To protect you in all your ways.
On their hands they will lift you up,
So that you do not strike your foot against a stone.
You will walk upon the lion and cobra,
You will trample the young lion and the serpent.
"Because he has loved Me, I will save him;
I will set him securely on high, because he has known My name.
He will call upon Me, and I will answer him;
I will be with him in trouble;
I will rescue him and honour him.
I will satisfy him with a long life,

And show him My salvation."

But even so, our adversary—the devil—can still get a foothold if you let him.

And on this particular evening at Long Beach, I was feeling the attack.

The family was being grumpy with one another; some things were said which cut deep. A trivial and meaningless something had grown arms and legs.

Stress, misunderstanding, and then silence pursued.

I cried out in my quiet thoughts to the Lord and asked for His mercy, peace, and grace to cover us that evening and for reconciliation to come in the morning.

My reading for that evening included a slightly different version:

In all circumstances, take up the shield of faith,
with which you can extinguish all the flaming
darts of the evil one. **Ephesians 6:16**

Those words that came from family members certainly felt like darts, Lord.
I repositioned my shield, turned the bedside light off, and closed my eyes.

The light shines in the darkness, and the
darkness has not overcome it. **John 1:5**

The following morning, the cloud appeared to have lifted (praise God), and a new and exciting day awaited us. After praying together as a couple, I put on my running clothes and headed out into the Long Island air to exercise.

I was still churning over the night before, forgiving those who had upset me and asking God to heal my heart. Spiritual warfare is very real, and it can often come full pelt—a swipe in your side from your nearest and dearest.

We need so much discernment, wisdom, and grace in these dark days. But,

The light is greater than the darkness. **John 1:5**

That simple phrase kept going over and over in my mind as I ran along the boardwalk that morning, smiling at fellow runners and watching and listening to the sea gently lap onto the golden sands. I saw a sign further up on the right hand side, and something in me made me stop to read it.

Long Beach Community Honors Dr. Martin
Luther King Jr. (1929-1968).

"Darkness cannot drive out darkness, only light can do
that, hate cannot drive out hate, only love can do that."

Jesus—You have to be kidding me.

Martin Luther King Jr. last visited Long Beach two weeks before he was assassinated in 1968, and every year on his birthday, the local residents march the same path that he marched with them.

He was a civil rights leader, committed to promoting equality and peace, regardless of race, culture, economic status, or ethnicity, and teaching people to love one another and to treat each other with dignity.

I stood there for a while, collecting my thoughts.

What was God trying to tell me?

On 1 December 1955 local National Association for the
Advancement of Colored People (NAACP) leader Rosa
Parks was arrested for refusing to give up her seat to a white

passenger on a city bus in Montgomery, Alabama. This single act of nonviolent resistance helped spark the Montgomery bus boycott, a 13-month struggle to desegregate the city's buses. Under the leadership of Martin Luther King, Jr., the boycott resulted in the enforcement of a U.S. Supreme Court ruling that public bus segregation is unconstitutional and catapulted both King and Parks into the national spotlight.[28]

Rosa Parks was a true freedom fighter of her time. She was prepared to commit civil disobedience for something she felt strongly about, and not only did it change US legislation, that simple act of peaceful non-compliance changed history.

The Bible has numerous accounts of standing up to power and authority when that authority is corrupt and ungodly.

Perhaps it's because I am a midwife that I am particularly fond of the story of the Hebrew midwives, Shiphrah and Puah (Exodus 1:15-21), who rejected any fear of man they may have had and did the Lord's work instead.

The king of Egypt had ordered the male Hebrew babies to be killed at birth, but the midwives refused to obey him.

When questioned about it, they made up an excuse that the Hebrew women gave birth quickly before they were able to arrive. God honoured the Hebrew midwives for fearing Him instead of man, and that simple act of civil disobedience allowed the birth of Moses to take place—the man who God chose to lead the Israelites out of slavery in Egypt and into the Promised Land.

Like Rosa Parks, these two women were history-makers for the kingdom of God and show us that speaking truth to power and standing up to corrupt and tyrannical authority is part of our call to faith.

---

28 Stanford University. (2023) Parks, Rosa.

Not to act is to act and God will not
hold us guiltless. **Eric Metaxas**

The theme of *freedom* seemed to be following me about—or is it that God goes before us and directs our steps?

Like Rosa Parks, Martin Luther King Jr., and many others I know and respect, I've been a *freedom fighter* too.

I'm not entirely sure I like that phrase because the only "fighting" is often done silently and always peacefully, but it has been a fight for freedom and our liberties all the same, and I have the battle scars to prove it.

Being a dissenter is certainly a sacrificial posture; long-established friendships may cease; you can be mocked and beaten in the new public square (online); people will try to deplatform you, even pull your mental health into question.

I'm sad to write this, but fellow believers, Christians, can be the worst for this.

You might even receive unjustified emails sent to your workplace and other ministry settings or offensive text messages sent to your mobile phone.

But if you only want to serve God and refuse to be intimidated by man, you have to expect and deal with the flood of abuse and attack you will inevitably receive. Jesus also knew what it was like to be wrongly accused, but He made this promise to us before He went to be with the Father:

> *"These things I have spoken to you, so that in Me you may*
> *have peace. In the world you have tribulation, but take*
> *courage; I have overcome the world."* **John 16:33**

I sat on a bench at Long Beach and looked out across the horizon.

I thought, *This is spiritual warfare.*

It's the battle of the mind and the battle for your soul.

It's the rough with the smooth.

The mountain tops and the valleys.

The twin-track life of blessings and pain, highs and lows, light and dark.

It's the knowing that *you're in the world, but you're not of it.*

It's the acceptance that we will experience trouble and tribulation in this world, but that Jesus has overcome it.

Hallelujah!

CHAPTER NINE

Everything will be okay in the end. If it's not okay, it's not the end.
John Lennon[29]

New York City, New York

Driving around Manhattan was an experience.

Although, unlike Central London, at least everything is one way.

Somebody once said, "The city is so nice, they named it twice." I think they were completely right about that.

Crossing over the Hudson River from the east side, I thought again about the Mayflower and how she was originally destined for New York but ended up docking at Plymouth, Massachusetts.

The following week, I was to be told about George Washington and his troops in 1776 making a miraculous escape across the East River and into Manhattan.

The British had failed to notice until it was too late.

Two days earlier, Americans had suffered a crushing defeat at Brooklyn Heights. That battle had ended with Washington's army cornered in Brooklyn.

---

[29] John Lennon, Good Reads *online*

Americans faced a problem: Their only escape route was across the East River, but such an escape was complicated by the presence of hundreds of British warships in the area. If the British saw the Americans escaping, these warships would be upon them very quickly.

On August 29th, Washington called a meeting with his generals. Brigadier General Thomas Mifflin, in charge of the Pennsylvania brigade, proposed a retreat across the East River during the night. He also proposed that his brigade take the most dangerous task: it would serve as rear guard. His brigade would be at the greatest risk, because it would be the last to leave.

Washington agreed. He had almost no choice. His army was weakened by the fact that it was split in half: Washington was with the soldiers in Brooklyn, but some of the army was still in Manhattan. The Brooklyn half of the army had little ammunition that had not been ruined by rain. An escape must be attempted, but the decision must be kept absolutely secret.

Word simply could not leak out.

At 7pm, the troops were told to pack up, but they were told they were preparing for a night attack on the enemy. Many of the soldiers thought the decision was rash, perhaps suicidal. Nevertheless, the least experienced troops, along with the sick and wounded, were soon ordered to the river. It had been raining all day and the current was so swift that the boats couldn't even attempt a crossing. The first round of troops simply stood there, in the dark, until 11pm, when the wind finally died down and the river became somewhat passable.

Throughout the night, the boats went back and forth in incredibly difficult conditions. Little by little, the troops on the lines were told to leave and head to the river. Throughout this time, Mifflin's brigade, on the outermost defenses, deliberately moved about, tending to campfires and such. They wanted it to appear that the army was still present and operating as normal.

Hours later, the retreat simply was not moving quickly enough. For a little while, it must have seemed that all was lost. Some historians relate a story about a panicked stampede onto the boats toward the end of the night. Reportedly, Washington hoisted a large rock above his head and ordered the men off. He'd "sink [the boat] to hell," he reportedly threatened, unless the soldiers got off the boat! They did.

Some historians doubt this part of the story. Washington had worked hard to control his legendary temper. Would he really have lost it in such a setting, with so much already at stake?

Either way, no one disputes what happened next.

A heavy fog settled over Brooklyn at daybreak. It was so thick that one soldier later said you "could scarcely discern a man at six yards distance."

Interestingly, there was no fog at all on the Manhattan side of the river. The last of Washington's men, including Mifflin and his brigade, were finally called to the river. Washington, too, had stayed to the end.

Washington's army completed its escape to New York at about 7am. The fog lifted shortly thereafter. Nine thousand men had crossed the river, all without arousing suspicion.

The army had gone from crushing defeat to miraculous escape in a matter of days.[30]

An example of divine intervention?

A miracle?

It sounded like it to me.

It reminded me of a similar story I'd heard in Israel, at the Golan Heights, of the Yom Kippur War miracle of 1973, where the Israeli forces had the victory over the Syrians against all odds. One account writes:

(Israeli) Commander David Yinni was in the process of pulling his troops out of a confrontation with the Syrian army when he realized that they were trapped in a minefield. Knowing it would take a miracle for them to make it out alive, the troops began crawling on their bellies while using their bayonets to try and find the mines without setting them off.

At some point, one of the soldiers uttered a heartfelt prayer. As the story goes, all of a sudden a windstorm blew in. The soldiers hunkered down until the storm subsided, and when it did, it had blown away so much of the dirt that the mines

---

[30] Tara Ross. (2023) *Americana.*

were exposed and the entire platoon managed to escape unharmed.[31]

This was a modern-day miracle similar to that experienced 200 years earlier on the eastern seaboard by George Washington.

There are so many accounts in the Bible of God intervening in war situations.

Joshua prays to God for the sun and the moon to stand still to give his troops more daylight during battle:

So the sun stood still, and the moon stopped, until the nation avenged themselves of their enemies. **Joshua 10:12-24**

And in the Book of 1 Samuel, the Lord sent supernatural confusion and a loud thunder upon the Philistines, they became so frightened that the Israelites were able to defeat them in battle.

The Lord is our Helper and He fights for His people.

Righteousness and justice are the foundation of [His] throne; mercy and truth go before [Him]. **Psalm 89:14**

God never changes.
He stays the same.
He is the unchangeable God.

Jesus Christ is the same yesterday, and today, and forever. **Hebrews 13:8**

Unexplained healings, breakthroughs, and miracles still happen today.

---

[31] VINnews. (2023) A Yom Kippur War Miracle.

I love New York City.

I love it in the spring, the fall, the summer, and winter.

We rode the subway and got bagels; we sat in Bryant Park with coffee and listened to buskers; we got the ferry over to Staten Island and strolled around Central Park; we went out to diners and restaurants, had cocktails on the rooftop bars, we were dazzled by the lights on Broadway, and saw the tourist sights, by day and by night.

In fact, we hardly stopped to breathe in the city that never sleeps, but what we saw in Times Square made us stop in our tracks.

A few days prior, I was made aware of an intimidating billboard which had been erected in Times Square for a well-known, recently released horror movie. It displayed in large neon letters the demon Lilith with the words, "Welcome to Hell–New York."

How pleasant.

The launch date set for, wait for it June 6, 2023–yes, that's "6," "6," and "6" (two times three equals six) for those wondering. Was that a coincidence or a deliberate move from the other side?

I later saw an article informing the readers that the movie had made $666 million dollars in revenue in the first week. Well, of course they did.

Evil is no longer being hidden away, is it?

It is all in plain sight if you have the eyes to see and ears to hear.

The antichrist spirit has crept into our libraries and education systems, our hospitals, our governments, our police force, our judicial systems, our media and journalism, our medical institutions and, of course, even our churches.

Are these the days which the Bible refers to as the "end times"?

Over the past few years alone, we have witnessed a steady incremental rise in wickedness and lawlessness, corruption, sexual immorality, depravity, apostasy in the Church, idolatry, and more. My grandparents, my spirit-filled grandfather, who only passed away a decade ago or so, would no longer recognise the world in which their grandchildren and great-grandchildren now live.

It's like the boiling frog syndrome. A metaphor describing how when our situation deteriorates gradually, we tend to adapt to these conditions instead of getting rid of them, until we are so weak, that we are no longer able to escape.

Our world is asleep at the wheel.

On our penultimate morning in New York City, we decided to seize the opportunity and go up to the eighty-sixth floor of the Empire State Building to admire the panoramic views across the city in all four directions. I knew this would be a particularly challenging day for my husband who, from a specific acquired trauma in his life, had developed a fear of heights, and standing close to the edge of a very tall building would be difficult for him—but he was convicted to do it anyway and overcome that fear he had.

Christians are called to be overcomers:

> *For God has not given us a spirit of fear, but of power and of love and of a sound mind.* **2 Timothy 1:7**

Jesus overcame death at the cross; God overcame Satan:

> *And they overcame him because of the blood of the Lamb and because of the word of their testimony, and they did not love their life even when faced with death.* **Revelation 12:11**

And despite, at times, the quaking knees and the sweaty palms – my husband did it.

He didn't know it at the time, but this day was to be a significant event in his own story of betrayal, pain, brokenness, healing, restoration, and transformation.

God is faithful.

Harrogate, Yorkshire

We have been through our own battle where we needed a miracle to win.

It was December 2017.

Life was just chugging along, like it does.

I had noticed that my husband was acting a bit different.

He was a bit more stressed and anxious than usual.

He continued to be like this into 2018, and then in March 2018–*boom!*

This man that I shared my life with–a highly successful and well-respected man in the financial sector, deeply loved by all that knew him–suddenly became very ill. He had excessive pressures and stresses at work and was diagnosed with severe anxiety and depression.

Despite having worked in mental health, I'm afraid I had not read the signs.

Our whole world fell apart.

And this valley in our family life didn't just go on for two weeks or six weeks or even six months–but for two and a half long and painful years.

I had decided to leave my midwifery career only two weeks beforehand, and during this time, the Lord would strip everything away from us.

My husband, who only days before was running a business and making decisions all day long, could no longer answer if he wanted a cup of tea or coffee. The change in him was sudden and extremely worrying.

What was going to happen?

After a few weeks, I realised that we would be ok. My husband was the managing director of an insurance business, and he had benefits that would look after him (and our family) if this was a serious and long-term illness—or so I thought.

The medical insurance provider that he had paid into for years refused to pay out, and so, we went over nine months of a year without any income at all.

We trusted the world and the system, and guess what? They did all they could to destroy us, and the process they put us through was incredibly painful.

We employed a lawyer, who implied that we would need a miracle to win.

We had no choice but to trust in God and His plan and purpose for our lives.

The Bible, the Living Word, is unchanging—centuries old and bursting with scripture relevant to all kinds of situations we might face, including the one we were facing right now.

*Even though I walk **through** the valley of the shadow of death, I fear no evil for you are with me.* **Psalm 23:1**

So do not worry about tomorrow; for tomorrow will worry about itself. **Matthew 6:34**

Trust in the Lord with all your heart and do not lean on your own understanding. **Proverbs 3:5**

"Do not fear or be dismayed because of this great multitude, for the battle is not yours but God's." **2 Chronicles 20:15**

You see, there are some battles we can't even try to fight in our own strength. These battles are totally out of our control, and mental illness is one of them.

It's unpredictable and often relentless, cruel, and destructive.

The recovery period is just as painful and uncertain, and there is the added pressures of relationship breakdown, financial difficulties, emotional distress, and the wider family fallout.

And so, the battle is no longer just a health battle, as challenging as that is – it becomes so much more than that – a battle for survival.

It becomes a joy stealer, and it runs you into the ground. It tries to break you.

This is what spiritual warfare is.

But when we have Jesus, the Son of God, on our side, *nothing is impossible.*

When we have the God Almighty and His angel armies fighting for us, *then nothing can be against us.*

If God is for us, who is against us? **Romans 8:31**

For *the battle belongs to God,* and we don't have to fight it by ourselves. We just need to *stand firm.*

We give thanks and honour to our brothers and sisters in Christ and to our non-Christian friends, the "people of peace," who prayed for us, loved us, and supported us through that difficult period in our lives.

And I give thanks to Him, the Wonderful Counsellor, the Prince of Peace, for the power of prayer and His continual presence.

God provided for us in so many different ways.

People around us began to wonder, *How can they have peace and continue to live their lives to the fullest while they have all this pain going on?*

We had to humble ourselves and go low.

We had nothing left of us—only our faith, which we clung onto by our fingernails.

But the *Lord* spoke so loud and clear to us during that time, and we saw many miracles too. God is a faithful God, and He always turns up when you surrender to Him in humility and complete dependence.

I remember going running one morning, and I was asking, pleading with the Lord, *How much longer?*

And as I turned a corner, I saw a sign in the road where some workmen were doing some local pipe work. It read, *"Short-term disruption, long-term benefits."*

We then kept seeing similar signs all across the town and even in different parts of the country.

I also recall one Sunday evening when we had done all that we could, but we knew that we were still unable to pay our mortgage the following day.

We got down on our knees and cried out to God again:*"We just do not know what to do, God, but we trust You. You've done it before, God, and we know that You will do it again. Our eyes are upon You."*

And then the phone rang.

It was a couple who we had only known for a short time.

"You are on our hearts," they said. "Is everything ok?"

We told them our desperate situation, and they sorted it immediately.

What an answer to prayer.

Then the phone rang again. It was another couple that we had only known for a short time.

"You are on our hearts," they said. "Is everything ok?"

We told them the situation and the immediate answer to prayer. They said, "It is great that you can pay your mortgage, but we want to bless you and your family at this time".

Before we knew it, they had blessed us financially, and we instantaneously went from praying on our knees in pain, to praying on our knees in joy and giving thanks to the Lord.

God provided over and over again.

There are so many remarkable stories and miracles from this time, but this is my husband's story. I hope he gets the chance to tell it someday.

That moment for me was the Valley of the Shadow of Death (which David talks about in Psalm 23), the Pit of Despair—the most frightening and desperate part.

The Kidron Valley in Israel separates the Temple Mount from the Mount of Olives in Jerusalem.

The reason it's called the Valley of the Shadow or the Valley of Death is because it is constantly in shadow, and the Psalmist used that valley as an example to represent the painful challenges of life from which God protects and guides believers. But the Bible says that the Lord takes us *through* the valleys of life—He doesn't leave us there. We just need to trust Him, and He delivers us safely to the other side.

God is always faithful.

The legal battle carried on until July 2020, but we did not let it consume us.

We trusted in God for His deliverance, we praised Him when it came, and we thanked Him for the miraculous healing and restoration that followed.

New York City, New York

Walking up Park Avenue in midtown New York City, the large letters of the medical insurance company provider that had caused us so much pain loomed in front of us like a modern-day version of the Tower of Babel.

I wondered how my husband would react. I didn't point it out to him, but I could tell that he had seen it.

But we were not shaken.

God has graciously healed and restored us both.

I couldn't help but smile at the street name directly in front of me, whose cross-shaped signage stood tall in front of the large shining letters that had caused us nothing but pain: *"Lighthouse Way."*

Another God Wink.

As we crossed over the next street, the road suddenly became closed, and NYPD officers were standing all over the place.

"Excuse me, ma'am. You need to stay on this side; the president is on his way."

"The president of the United States of America?"

"Yes ma'am, the president."

I suddenly remembered my casual prayer at the beginning of the trip to see somebody with influence and power and have the opportunity to pray for them.

I could hardly believe it.

Of all the streets, of all the corners, of all the days, of all the hours.

But God.

So, I prayed, and I prayed, and I prayed!

CHAPTER TEN

If freedom of speech is taken away, then dumb and silent we may be led, like sheep to the slaughter.
George Washington[32]

Washington D.C.

The following afternoon, we took the AMTRAK train from Pennsylvania Station in New York City through to Union Street Station in Washington, D.C.

It was a beautiful journey through New Jersey, Pennsylvania, Delaware, and Maryland, crossing waterways and large cities, farmland and woodland.

On the way, we tuned in to the UK evening news to watch a clergy friend of ours speak about his savings bank account being threatened with closure due to his orthodox Christian viewpoint on sexuality issues.

The calendar had now turned to July, but when we arrived in Washington, D.C., we were reminded that June had only just passed, and one would still need to embrace the cultural celebrations of the month (pride month) whether one wanted to or not.

We didn't want to do it, but that didn't seem to matter.

Tough.

---

[32] George Washington, Good Reads *online*

Speaking of such, I recalled what happened overnight in New York City.

On June 30, the banks, many of the grand hotels, the iconic New York City Library, and even a number of churches had bowed the knee to a false god. The Rockefeller Centre on 5th Avenue had gone even further and exchanged every United States of America flag with the alternative LGBTQ flag; even the toy shops were joining in! It was as if a foreign nation had invaded and occupied the country.

But on July 1, it was all stripped away in the blink of an eye and replaced once more with the stars and stripes.

Here today, gone tomorrow in the twinkling of an eye. It was all over.

How much more do we believers long for the coming return of King Jesus, when only one thing shall remain forever – the Lord Himself.

> *In a moment, in the twinkling of an eye, at the last trumpet; for the trumpet will sound, and the dead will be raised imperishable, and we will be changed.* **1 Corinthians 15:52**

We knew that we had fairly limited time in the US Capitol, and so, that particular day had similarities to *National Lampoon's Vacation*[33] and a frantic Chevy Chase on his way to Wally World: "*There's the White House kids! Lincoln's Memorial—tick! Quick family photo outside Capitol Hill—snap! Stop dawdling, you lot!*"

It was about 35 degrees in the shade, and I couldn't work out if I was sweating into a puddle from the humidity or from rushing around like a blue-ass fly.

I'm guessing it was both.

God gave us some precious moments too, despite behaving like over-keen tourists.

---

[33] National Lampoon's Vacation (1983)

I noticed that they were putting up a big stage on Constitution Avenue and closing roads left, right, and centre.

"Hey, what's going on?" I asked a man from the Metropolitan Police Department sitting in his vehicle with a coffee, watching the proceedings.

"There's *always* something going on in D.C.," he replied with a kind smile. "It's probably something to do with July 4."

"Of course, we're in July," I remembered.

The officer got out of his car, and we started to talk on the sidewalk. He was called M.E. Johnson, and he was working after retirement. I hope he reads this book one day because that conversation was an unexpected blessing for me.

I honestly can't recall how the conversation flowed from one hot topic to the next, but I know that the Lord was with us as we spoke, and it was wonderful to find a brother in Christ of likeminded spirit and discernment in a place which felt, in many ways, like the *Belly of the Beast*.

An unforgettable Holy-Spirit-led and divine moment of conversation, laughter, and prayer. We stood together declaring God's reign and rule over the Land of the Free; we pushed back the darkness and satanic agendas and raised a banner of righteousness over the city of Washington, D.C.!

When the enemy comes in like a flood, the Spirit of the Lord will lift up a standard against him. **Isaiah 59:19**

It was a Sunday, so we called into David's Tent by the National Mall to worship.

We visited the Smithsonian National Museum of Natural History.

We sat on a bench in the sunshine, people-watched, and ate ice cream.

We walked past the Sylvan Theatre and listened to a woman speaking out about the New World Order, the Mark of the Beast, and the end times.

I prayed for an evangelist giving out Christian tracts by the Lincoln Memorial Pool, and then we went back to the hotel and sunbathed by the pool, drinking Pina Coladas before dinner.

That evening, we went back into town for round two.

Exploring Washington, D.C., by night is a real treat—not only is it quieter, but there's a deeper stillness and a peace that doesn't seem to be present in the daytime.

> *Things are not always what they seem; the first appearance deceives many; the intelligence of a few perceives what has been carefully hidden.* **Phaedrus**

Washington, D.C., is another place of high supernatural energy, much like what we experienced in Martha's Vineyard. For those who are spiritually aware of the realm of angelic and demonic forces, there are ungodly powers and principalities at play that have no doubt occupied the place because of a political spirit of dominance and control, adhering to worldly cultural agendas rather than clinging to the life-giving Word of God as the moral compass.

You can feel it as you walk the streets.

There is much going on under the surface of what we see.

Things are not always what they seem; the first appearance deceives many.

Deception and *falsehood* are words which cover many deceptive practices. Uttering lies, practicing deceit, bearing false witness, lying, and using smooth talk or flattery to deceive somebody else are just some of the sinister methods. It is a spirit, and like Satan himself, it can appear as an *angel of light*; deception is very confusing. It's normally *almost right*, which makes it even harder to see to the unsuspecting or undiscerning eye.

There is a thick spirit of deception both in the world and in the Church today.

It has often felt like a fog of confusion, lethargy, and hypnosis took over the world at the beginning of 2020 and perhaps it hasn't lifted yet.

This has all helped to usher in the spirit of deception.

To understand deception, you also need to understand the spirit of Pan.

Caesarea Philippi, Israel, BC

Originally known as *Banias*, Caesarea Philippi was situated twenty-five miles (forty kilometers) north of the Sea of Galilee and at the base of Mt. Hermon. It was a city of Greek-Roman culture known for its worship of foreign gods.

The people honoured and worshipped the Greek god Pan—a half-man, half-goat deity, often depicted playing a flute. Much depravity, debauchery, and sadistic rituals went on there amongst the Pagan believers.

It was there that Jesus chose to take His disciples and announced He would establish His Church and gave authority over it to the apostle Simon, whom He renamed Peter:

> *"And I also say to you that you are Peter, and upon this rock I will build My church; and the gates of Hades will not overpower it."* **Matthew 16:18**

He called it *the gates of Hell* for good reason.

I visited the archaeological remains in 2022, and there was a dark presence felt even then. It was interesting to hear about the god of Pan from our tour guide. He, too, had witnessed the deception and confusion that was covering the earth the past few years, and he went on to explain about the spirit of Pan.

Pan was half-man, half-goat because the worshippers practised beastiality. This is where we get the root of the words such as *"pandemic," "panic,"* and *"pandemonium."*

He played a flute, which invoked a deep lethargy and hypnosis; they were unable to see truth and lived under a veil of deception and lies.

Imagine Mr, Tumnus in *The Lion, the Witch and the Wardrobe* (C.S. Lewis)[34].

"You see—different day, different century, but the same spirit," our guide said.

Some things were starting to make perfect sense.

Washington, D.C.

I've realised that for all of my life, I've been deceived by the size of the White House. It always looks so big, full of grandeur, and imposing on the TV or in newspapers, yet in reality, it's really quite small and underwhelming.

"All the English say that," the security guard said to me.

I smiled back.

Things are not as they seem.

> There is an evil which I have seen under the sun, and
> it is widespread among mankind: a person to whom
> God has given riches, wealth, and honour, so that
> his soul lacks nothing of all that he desires, yet God
> has not given him the opportunity to enjoy these
> things, but a foreigner enjoys them. This is futility
> and a severe affliction. **Ecclesiastes 6:1-2**

---

[34] The Lion, the Witch and the Wardrobe (C.S. Lewis, 2009)

The intelligence of a few perceives what has been carefully hidden.

The Bible speaks about the gift of *discernment* – that is, to have a supernatural and instinctive gift to know the difference between a truth and a lie, good from evil, right and wrong, or a good teacher and a false prophet. It is a spiritual gift to know the difference between different spirits, and it is a kind of wisdom that comes from insight as much as from learned experience and knowledge.

> *But solid food is for the mature, who because of*
> *practice have their senses trained to distinguish*
> *between good and evil.* **Hebrews 5:14**

Discernment is a gift from God that is given His to believers from the Holy Spirit, and not all people appear to have it.

> *But a natural person does not accept the things of*
> *the Spirit of God, for they are foolishness to him;*
> *and he cannot understand them, because they are*
> *spiritually discerned.* **1 Corinthians 2:14**

Scripture tells us to set our eyes on things above—the things that are not seen and not of this world, rather than what we can only see with our earthly eyes:

> *While we look not at the things which are seen, but*
> *at the things which are not seen; for the things*
> *which are seen are temporal, but the things which*
> *are not seen are eternal.* **2 Corinthians 4:18**

I believe we need to have discernment more than ever in these days.

The end time deception is a biblical narrative that refers to the widespread influence of falsehood and deception, counterfeit miracles, and false prophets in the last days; one of the main deceivers being the antichrist himself.

Like every false messiah before him, the antichrist will convince his followers he is the answer to the world's problems. The apostle Paul tells us that those who become caught in the antichrist's web of deceit will be guilty because they freely choose to enjoy evil while denying the truth:

> *And with all the deception of wickedness for those who perish, because they did not accept the love of the truth so as to be saved. For this reason God will send upon them a deluding influence so that they will believe what is false, in order that they all may be judged who did not believe the truth, but took pleasure in wickedness.* **2 Thessalonians 2:10-12**

Things are not always what they seem; the first appearance deceives many; the intelligence of a few perceives what has been carefully hidden.[35]

---

[35] Phaedrus, Good Reads *online*

CHAPTER ELEVEN

We hold these truths to be self-evident, that all men are created equal, that they are endowed by their Creator with certain inalienable rights, among these are life, liberty, and the pursuit of happiness, that to secure these rights governments are instituted among men.
Thomas Jefferson[36]

After visiting family in Washington, D.C., we travelled the 150-mile journey down through Virginia and arrived with special friends in Williamsburg.

The Historic Triangle includes three historic colonial communities located on the Virginia Peninsula of the United States and is bounded by the York River in the north and the James River in the south. The points that form the triangle are Jamestown, Colonial Williamsburg, and Yorktown.

Jamestown, Virginia

On December 6, 1606, the journey to Virginia began on three ships: the *Susan Constant,* the *Godspeed,* and the *Discovery.* In 1607, 104 English men and boys arrived in North America to start a settlement, and on May 13, they picked Jamestown, Virginia, for their settlement, named after King

---

36 Thomas Jefferson, Good Reads *online*

James I. The settlement became the first permanent English settlement in North America.

The site for Jamestown was picked for several reasons, all of which met criteria for the Virginia Company, who funded the settlement. The site was surrounded by water on three sides (it was not fully an island yet) and was far inland; both meant it was easily defendable against possible Spanish attacks.

The water was also deep enough that the English could tie their ships at the shoreline, and the site was also not inhabited by the Native population.

Today, Jamestown Island is a historic site, though there is still a private residence on the island.[37]

Colonial Williamsburg, Virginia

The city of Williamsburg was founded as the capital of the Virginia Colony in 1699, and it was here that the basic concepts of the United States of America were formed under the leadership of George Washington, Thomas Jefferson, George Mason, and many others.

Named "Williamsburg" in honour of England's reigning monarch at the time, King William III, the city also became a centre of learning. The College of William and Mary was founded in 1693 and counts political leaders such as Presidents Thomas Jefferson, James Monroe, and John Tyler as alumni.

During its time as the capital of Virginia, Williamsburg flourished as the hub of religious, economic, and social life in the state. A palatial Governor's Palace was built, as were markets, taverns, a theatre, Bruton Parish Church (those living in the New World were required by law to worship in the Church of England), and countless homes.

---

[37] National Park Service. (2022) *Historic Jamestowne*

Following the Declaration of Independence from Britain, however, the American Revolutionary War broke out, and the capital of Virginia was moved fifty miles (80.4 kilometers) north to Richmond. It was feared that Williamsburg's location allowed easy access for the British to attack.

The United States of America's independence from Great Britain was a turning point in world history.[38]

Yorktown, Virginia

Yorktown was established by the Act for Ports of 1691, passed by the General Assembly at Jamestown (Virginia's government seat for almost a century). The legislation was but another in a succession of disputed and unsuccessful efforts by the colonial government to encourage growth of towns in rural Tidewater, Virginia. Yorktown, however, succeeded despite initial delays and frustrations.

Fifty acres of land along the York River for the site of Yorktown were purchased from Benjamin Read of Gloucester County (across the York River from Yorktown) for 10,000 pounds of "merchantable sweet, scented tobacco and cask."

In a few years, the town began to take root. The better homes, inns, and public buildings were developed on the river bluff, while "York under the hill" (the waterfront) featured wharves, warehouses, small stores, and lodging and drinking places. The York County Courthouse was built about 1697, and the York Parish Church was built in 1697, becoming the area's religious centre. Both were key institutions in the new community.

The siege of Yorktown, also known as the Battle of Yorktown, was the last major land battle of the American Revolutionary War in North America.

---

[38] The Culture Trip. (2023) *A Brief History of Colonial Williamsburg, Virginia*

The Continental Army's victory at Yorktown prompted the British government to negotiate an end to the conflict.[39]

We explored the Historic Triangle on the fourth of July–America's Independence Day.

As a British girl, I found this slightly uncomfortable at first.

After all, should I really be celebrating that we, the British, got defeated?

Truth be told, my American history was rather poor prior to the trip, and I hadn't really contemplated the significance, but I did feel an overwhelming sense of the Lord's presence as I walked around the three sites.

What would God teach me through this?

We visited Bruton Parish Church in Colonial Williamsburg, and I felt goosebumps. The presence of the Holy Spirit felt tangible in that place. A well-preserved traditional parish church that looked like it had been uprooted from England and placed down on American soil. As I looked at the wooden pews with familiar names inscribed onto each one, *General George Washington* and *Thomas Jefferson*, to name a couple, and I beheld the ornate pulpit, I pondered upon all the stories the stone walls could share with me if only they could speak.

When the English colony was established at Jamestown on May 14, 1607, the conduct of worship and the building of a primitive chapel were given priority even as the first fort was built. The Reverend Robert Hunt served as the first chaplain. He had been the chaplain appointed to serve as spiritual leader of the three-ship expedition headed by Christopher Newport.

Captain John Smith described the Reverend Robert Hunt as *our honest, religious and courageous divine*. In his role as religious leader, he was a peacemaker, often bringing

---

[39] National Park Service. (2022) *Yorktown Battlefield*

harmony to a quarrelling group of men. Sadly, Hunt was among those who did not survive that first year.

The expansion and subdivision of the church parishes and shires (counties) of Virginia after 1634 both followed this growth. Parishes needed to be close enough for travel to church for worship, an obligation everyone was expected to fulfil.[40]

The tour guide told us that Bruton (named after the town of Bruton in the County of Somerset, England, the hometown of Thomas Ludwell, secretary of the colony, and Governor William Berkeley) was one of many Church of England parishes established in the colonies. After the American Revolution severed official ties to England, these parishes organised themselves as the Episcopal Church while remaining part of the worldwide Anglican Communion. It is still a living and vibrant Episcopal church today, serving a parish of about 2,000 members.

This was the fourth of July, and the U.S. citizens were celebrating their Independence Day.

On July 4, 1776, the thirteen New World colonies, those that were considered subjects of the King of England, declared their independence from Britain's Parliament as well as King George III himself.

America had finally won their freedom from what they had felt to be an enslavement to English rule and reign. Over time, more and more of the colonists began to resent being under the thumb of Great Britain. This tension turned to outrage when the British Parliament imposed the Stamp Act in 1765, putting a tax directly onto the colonists for the first time.

I guess they thought, *"Enough is enough."*

I know how that feels.

---

[40] Wikipedia. (2023) *Bruton Parish Church*

I began to genuinely understand their plight and predicament for the first time in my life and repented of feeling all pompous, elitist, and British about it.

Of course they'd wanted independence; they were finally standing up to corruption, greed, enslavement, tyranny, and governmental overreach.

I understood their concerns and their struggles, and that evening, we celebrated under the warm Williamsburg skies watching the firework display with friends.

The words from the Book of Ecclesiastes landed hard into my soul:

What has been, it is what will be, and what has been done, it is what will be done. So there is nothing new under the sun. **Ecclesiastes 1:9**

History has a tendency to repeat itself, or as the philosopher George Santayana put it, *"Those who cannot remember the past, are condemned to repeat it."*

There is nothing new under the sun. The Bible has countless stories of tyranny, disobedience, greed, the evil deeds of man, the worship of false idols, and the celebration of ungodly and unrighteous living.

All of these accounts end in tribulation, great suffering, and judgement.

For you have not received a spirit of slavery leading to fear again, but you have received a spirit of adoption as sons and daughters by which we cry out, "Abba! Father!" **Romans 8:15**

I had written a talk in early June for a Filling Station meeting I was speaking at in Smithfield, Virginia, on Saturday, July 8, 2023, and when I asked the Lord what message I needed to share, He gave me that verse in Romans as a pin.

I started to see an even greater significance to the Word than I had before.

God is so kind to us like that.

Just like layers of an onion, He often reveals new things to us in stages—a fresh revelation of His Word or a new interpretation of something we have heard.

The Bible speaks a lot about freedom and that knowing Jesus Christ and being set free by the power of the Holy Spirit is the only way to be completely free.

For you were called to freedom, brothers (and sisters). **Galatians 5:13**

It was for freedom that Christ set us free; therefore, keep standing firm and do not be subject again to a yoke of slavery. **Galatians 5:1**

And I will walk at liberty, For I seek Your precepts. **Psalm 119:45**

So if the Son sets you free, you really will be free. **John 8:36**

The world wants to enslave us, but God wants us to live freely.

If you're reading this and you are feeling, trapped, worthless, let down, persecuted, depressed, heavily-laden, or completely desperate because of your current situation—wherever you are, whatever you're doing, ask Jesus, the Son of God, to come into your heart as your Lord, God, and Saviour and set you completely free.

He is just a breath away.

I promise.

CHAPTER TWELVE

Almost heaven, West Virginia
Blue ridge mountains, Shenandoah river
Life is old there, older than the trees
Younger than the mountains, blowing like a breeze
Country roads, take me home
To the place I belong
West Virginia, mountain mamma
Take me home, country roads.
John Denver[41]

Wintergreen, Virginia

The next two days were spent up in the Blue Ridge Mountains of Virginia.

It had been a crazy twelve days living life in the fast lane, and we'd put these nights on the schedule to give us time to rest, reflect, and restore.

As we drove along those country roads, we saw the landscape change ahead of us—the farmland, the streams, the large ranches with their acres of land, the watering holes, the architecture, even the colours of the trees in the hazy sunshine seemed to bring a different perspective to what we'd seen before.

---

[41] Lyrics STANDS4 LLC. (2023) *"Country Road" Kobalt Music Publishing Ltd/ Bill Danoff, John Denver, Taffy Nivert Danoff.*

And then, stretching ahead of us, was the beauty and majesty of the Blue Ridge Mountains, becoming closer and closer until we were cocooned inside of them.

My soul was at rest.

The mountains are a special place for me and help me to connect spiritually.

The crisp air filling my lungs.

The sound of water streaming down on the falls.

The birds singing over me.

The smell of nature at its best; the bark, the flowers, the forest dew.

The silent pause.

The crunch of the woodland path beneath my exploring feet, and the movement of the branches of the trees gently swaying in the wind.

It was a time to be with each other, to be with God, and to just . . . be.

Stop striving and know that I am God. **Psalm 46:10**

There are numerous accounts in the Bible where Jesus left the busyness of life to spend time alone in nature with His Father. Jesus was and is the true representation of God the Father, and so, everything He did and said was to set the example for us.

And like Jesus, we need to intentionally get away every so often to a quiet place and meet with God—to restore our soul, to open our ears to hear His voice, and to allow the Lord to speak into our very being and bring healing and guidance.

Jesus said to the people:

*"Come to Me, all who are weary and burdened, and
I will give you rest. Take My yoke upon you and learn*

*from Me, for I am gentle and humble in heart, and you
will find rest for your souls. For My yoke is comfortable,
and My burden is light."* **Matthew 11:28-30**

The Lord gave me two divine encounters in the Blue Ridge Mountains—
one that rescued me, and one that marked me. Let me explain some more.

Rescue

Wintergreen is a four-season resort, and in early July, it seemed to be unusually quiet. Known in the state of Virginia for its skiing and winter-sports, it is equally enjoyed by mountain-lovers and hikers in the warmer months. We took a drive up to the Devil's Knob Loop—an interesting name—but apparently called as such because when the first settlers discovered the land, certain parts were impassable and treacherous.

We were trying to find the start of a particular trail but were unsuccessful.

There was nobody around, and quite frankly, at this point, I was feeling hungry and getting more and more concerned about the black bears which roam freely around the place than doing anymore hiking in the forest with my family.

Lord, please help us out of this situation. We're lost.

We were standing at a viewing point, which overlooks the valley, and were about to give up when a middle-aged couple appeared from nowhere.

We started talking.

They owned a vacation home close to the top and were out on a spontaneous late afternoon stroll.

They said they knew the trail we wanted to accomplish because they had done it the day before. They also gave us a better route.

We soon discovered that they were both spirit-filled Christians – and we had mutual friends who lived in the UK.

I don't know about you, but I don't think that was a coincidence. In fact, I came to the conclusion many years ago that the God of Heaven doesn't do coincidences.

He heard my quiet, prayerful cry for help, and He executed His rescue plan.

Mark

After this encounter, we continued on our ambitious trek and finally found the trail path to the Upper Shamokin Falls and Gorge. Upon descent, I managed to slip on a stone and scrape the back of my right leg (just above my ankle line).

I'm a strong girl with tenacity from Yorkshire, but it did really hurt.

I washed it in the waterfalls, and the glorious sight of these falls took my mind off my injury, and I was able to climb back up on the other side without further calamity.

A couple of days later whilst showering, I noticed that the scar on my leg was in fact five inch-long scars that were in a line with one another and looked like tiny stripes on my lower calf muscle. The wound had cut so deep that the scarring looked like it would be there forever.

I had been marked.

I immediately thought of the prophetic word my friend Simon had given me about somehow being *marked* on this trip. I was being marked in so many ways emotionally and spiritually–now, I had a physical marking too.

It reminded me of a beautiful scripture from the Book of Isaiah –

But He was pierced for our offenses, He was crushed for our wrongdoings; The punishment for our well-being was laid upon Him, and by His wounds we are healed. **Isaiah 53:5**

In the King James Version of the Bible, it says:

And with his stripes we are healed. **Isaiah 53:5**

This whole afternoon experience, this *moment* with God in the beautiful Blue Ridge mountains, all felt like it had been perfectly ordained in advance for me.

He had brought me here to heal me and restore me.

God is my Rescuer and my Deliverer. And when we call on Him, He hears our prayers in Heaven, and He will do it:

> *Therefore, I say to you, all things for which you pray*
> *and ask, believe that you have received them, and*
> *they will be granted to you.* **Mark 11:24**

I am *marked* or sealed by His Holy Spirit.

And that by His *stripes* I am healed.

Jesus still heals today.

If you're reading this and you are needing to receive healing in any way for your mind, body, or spirit, wherever you are, whatever you're doing, ask Jesus, the Son of God, to come by His Spirit and heal you.

He is just a breath away.

I promise.

That evening, we snuggled up in our vacation rental and watched the movie *Evan Almighty (2007)*. It is set in Virginia and is a modern-day retelling of Noah's Ark, which Evan Baxter, pursuing a new career in local government, reluctantly re-enacts because God commands him to do so.

I'm sorry to ruin the movie if you haven't seen it, but the ark finally gets built, and the flood does eventually come, wiping out the entire valley of housing—all because a corrupt and greedy congressman had decided to cost-cut and had tried to pass an unlawful public land act, which led to the dam's failure.

I'm sure nothing like that would ever happen in real life politics . . .

The words of the classic John Denver song "Country Road" stayed in my head for much of that visit to the Blue Ridge mountains. It was *almost* Heaven up there, or at least, how one might imagine Heaven to be.

And one day, as believers in Christ, we will be "going home"– going home to where we truly belong. I've never felt so out of place on this earth as I have over the past few years. Scripture tells us that we are temporary residents here–sojourners, foreigners, strangers, and aliens–and that our home, our eternal dwelling place, is in Heaven.

> *Beloved, I urge you as foreigners and strangers*
> *to abstain from fleshly lusts, which wage*
> *war against the soul.* **1 Peter, 2:11**

> *They are not of the world, just as I am not of the*
> *world. Sanctify them in the truth; Your word is*
> *truth. Just as You sent Me into the world, I also*
> *sent them into the world.* **John 17:16-18**

Jesus said when talking about Heaven:

> *"Do not let your heart be troubled; believe in God,*
> *believe also in Me. In My Father's house are many*
> *rooms; if that were not so, I would have told you,*
> *because I am going there to prepare a place for*
> *you. And if I go and prepare a place for you, I am*
> *coming again and will take you to Myself, so that*
> *where I am, there you also will be."* **John 14:1-3**

Christians need to have double vision.

They are required to be *as wise as serpents* (Matthew 10:16), discerning the signs of the times and keeping their minds set on things above, which have eternal consequences, whilst navigating life and all its challenges and blessings here below.

We are not of this world, but we have been chosen by God to be in it.

As the world appears to be getting darker, know that the light of Jesus will always be brighter than the darkness, and it will continue to shine brighter and brighter until the Lord, our King Jesus, returns in all His glory.

And the Light shines in the darkness, and the darkness did not comprehend it. **John 1:5**

CHAPTER THIRTEEN

All the ends of the world shall remember and turn unto the Lord: and all the kindreds of the nations shall worship before thee. For the kingdom is the Lord's: and he is the governor among the nations.

Psalm 22:27-28

Virginia Beach, Virginia

Feeling adequately rested and restored, we left the mountains in the western part of Virginia, and we headed off toward the eastern seaboard and Virginia Beach, stopping off that evening in Smithfield to share with the local Filling Station Ministry there and to have fellowship with the team.

The Holy Spirit was present in a powerful way, and people were healed and delivered. It was a privilege to minister on the other side of the pond with treasured friends, and it felt like an outworking of those declarations made by the pilgrim fathers.

> After four and a half months crossing storm swept seas 144 weary Englishmen made land-fall in April 1607. They anchored their ships in the protected waters of the bay and landed a small party upon the shore. They built a wooden cross and planted it in the sand naming the place Cape Henry.

This is the first landing site of those adventurous Englishmen who, some three weeks later, established the first permanent English Colony in North America at Jamestown. A memorial cross of granite was erected in 1935 by the Daughters of the American Colonists to commemorate the site where a wooden cross was erected by those early adventurers in the spring of 1607.

Reverend Robert Hunt (c. 1568-1608), clergyman of the Church of England, was Chaplain of the expedition that founded Jamestown, Virginia. The expedition included people from Old Heathfield, East Sussex, England. The Reverend Hunt had become the Vicar of Heathfield, County of Sussex, in 1602, which title he held as Chaplain of the Jamestown Settlement.

He had previously been Vicar of Reculver, County of Kent, England, 1594-1602. He lit the candle for the Anglican Church in Virginia (United States) and he first lifted his voice in public thanksgiving and prayer on April 29, 1607, when the settlers planted a cross at Cape Henry, which they named after the Prince of Wales.[42]

Hunt declared this promise in front of God at Cape Henry, Virginia:

We do hereby dedicate this Land, and ourselves, to reach the People within these shores with the Gospel of Jesus Christ, and to raise up Godly generations after us, and with these generations take the Kingdom of God to all the earth. May

---

[42] National Park Service. (2022) *Cape Henry Memorial*

this Covenant of Dedication remain to all generations, as long as this earth remains and may this land, along with England, be evangelists to the world.

May all who see this cross remember what we have done here, and may those who come here to inhabit join us in this Covenant and this most noble work, that the Holy Scriptures may be fulfilled. From these very shores the gospel shall go forth, not only to this new world, but the entire world.[43]

After attending church on Sunday morning, we had arranged a family visit and cycle ride around the First Landings State Park. The kids weren't having any of it and opted for a swim and sleep instead! After initially feeling a little "mum-disappointment" that they didn't share the same enthusiasm as us about that, my husband and I decided to go on our own. In hindsight, of course, this was always meant to be the plan, and we can now see how God goes before us to create the optimum scenario.

In fact, it was perfect that it was just us.

Fort Story is a U.S. military base located at the entrance of the Chesapeake Bay within the city of Virginia Beach. It is the Army's only training facility for logistics-over-the-shore operations to train troops on amphibious equipment and to practice the transfer of military cargo from ship to shore.

Cape Henry is located within the confines of Fort Story, and so, it is quite literally a *military operation* to even get to it. You must show ID and be willing to be searched and questioned upon arrival, and there are very strict guidelines as to where you can go and what areas are restricted.

---

43 National Park Service. (2022) *Cape Henry Memorial*

I'm not sure what happens if you disregard these rules, but since the personnel were all carrying firearms, we listened up and took notice.

We saw the Cape Henry lighthouses before making our way to the memorial cross, which is naturally positioned very close to the shoreline.

It was hidden around a corner, and as I saw it, my heart filled up with a sense of love, and it felt like time was standing still. I can't really explain to you what happened in that moment, only how I felt.

An overwhelming, awesome sense of the Lord's presence came over me—a deep gratitude that I was even there—almost like if you've ever scaled a mountain to the top peak, submitted a dissertation, or completed running a marathon. *I made it, and this moment is significant in my life.*

It was a realisation that so many things had led me to this point.

Thoughts, pictures, and words painted an image in my mind of the historical moments that had been captured here—the first pilgrims placing their feet upon the sandy shore.

It was a deeply spiritual encounter—a supernatural collision in the heavenly realms and on the earth below—a sense this wasn't just a regular tourist visit out of curiosity; it was so much more than that.

This was God Himself who had lured us to this place *for such a time as this* (Esther 4:14).

I knelt in front of the cross and read the plaque in front of me:

HERE AT CAPE HENRY FIRST LANDED IN AMERICA, UPON 26 APRIL 1607, THOSE ENGLISH COLONIST WHO, UPON 13 MAY 1607, ESTABLISHED AT JAMESTOWN VIRGINIA, THE FIRST PERMANENT ENGLISH SETTLEMENT IN AMERICA.

Something happened in that moment for us both, and we were undone. I lay prostrate on the ground, face down, and poured out my heart to God.

I confessed my sins and repented of everything I had gotten wrong and on behalf of our people, our nation, our world.

I forgave where I needed to forgive.

I asked God to wipe the slate clean once more.

And just as the Pilgrim Fathers had driven that original wooden cross into the ground all those years ago and made an outwardly declaration to God to *"dedicate this Land"* and themselves *"to reach the People within these shores with the Gospel of Jesus Christ, and to raise up Godly generations after them, and with these generations take the Kingdom of God to all the earth,"*[44] so did we.

Like many before us, we made a covenant with the Lord that *"from these very shores the gospel shall go forth, not only to this new world,"* to the United States of America, *"but the entire world."*[45]

For we too are missionaries from England, evangelists to the world, bringing the gospel of Jesus Christ, the Good News.

And it is our prayer that *"this Covenant of Dedication remain to all generations, as long as this earth remains and may this land,"* the United States of America, *"along with England, be evangelists to the world."*[46]

Amen.

We stood up, and behind us were two young Americans in their twenties. We started to talk to them and immediately felt the Holy Spirit urge us to pray for them both. We spoke prophetically into their lives, and as we did, tears began to flow. We told them the way to salvation and asked God to show up in their lives in a profound way over the next few days.

The woman took a Christian tract that was hanging from a nearby tree, and we embraced and wished them well on their way.

It was a divine appointment.

---

[44] National Park Service. (2022) *Cape Henry Memorial Cross*

[45] IBID

[46] IBID

The covenant that we had just pledged together before the Lord at the memorial cross was already being birthed in the present.

Hallelujah!

> *And He said to them, "Go into all the world and preach the gospel to all creation. The one who has believed and has been baptized will be saved; but the one who has not believed will be condemned. These signs will accompany those who have believed: in My name they will cast out demons, they will speak with new tongues; they will pick up serpents, and if they drink any deadly poison, it will not harm them; they will lay hands on the sick, and they will recover."* **Mark 16:15-18**

CHAPTER FOURTEEN

It is no dishonour to be in a minority in the cause of liberty and virtue.
Samuel Adams[47]

Boston, Massachusetts

We flew back up to Boston, Massachusetts, from Richmond Airport for the final few days of our family vacation on the east coast of the United States.

My father travelled extensively when I was a youngster, and he had always remarked upon how Boston was his favourite place to visit. When I was a small child, I remember him buying me a stuffed scruffy dog toy from Boston on one of his many trips overseas, and I had excitedly named him after the city.

I treasured that dog, and I went to Boston with an expectant heart that God would speak to us once more in that place.

> The Boston Tea Party, (16th December, 1773), refers to an incident in which 342 chests of tea belonging to the British East India Company were thrown from ships into Boston Harbor by American patriots disguised as Mohawk Indians. The Americans were protesting both a tax on tea (taxation

---

[47] Samuel Adams, Good Reads *online*

without representation) and the perceived monopoly of the East India Company.

The Townshend Acts passed by Parliament in 1767 and imposing duties on various products imported into the British Colonies had raised such a storm of colonial protest and noncompliance that they were repealed in 1770, saving the duty on tea, which was retained by Parliament to demonstrate its presumed right to raise such colonial revenue without colonial approval. The merchants of Boston circumvented the act by continuing to receive tea smuggled in by Dutch traders.

In 1773, Parliament passed a Tea Act designed to aid the financially troubled East India Company by granting it (1) a monopoly on all tea exported to the colonies, (2) an exemption on the export tax, and (3) a "drawback" (refund) on duties owed on certain surplus quantities of tea in its possession. The tea sent to the colonies was to be carried only in East India Company ships and sold only through its own agents, bypassing the independent colonial shippers and merchants. The company thus could sell the tea at a less-than-usual price in either America or Britain; it could undersell anyone else. The perception of monopoly drove the normally conservative colonial merchants into an alliance with radicals led by Samuel Adams and his Sons of Liberty.

In such cities as New York, Philadephia and Charleston, tea agents resigned or cancelled orders, and merchants refused consignments. In Boston, however, the royal governor Thomas Hutchinson determined to uphold the law and maintained that three arriving ships, the *Dartmouth, Eleanor,* and

Beaver, should be allowed to deposit their cargoes and that appropriate duties should be honoured. On the night of the 16th December, 1773, a group of about 60 men, encouraged by a large crowd of Bostonians, donned blankets and Indian headdresses, marched to Griffin's wharf, boarded the ships, and dumped the tea chests, valued at £18,000, into the water.

In retaliation, Parliament passed the series of punitive measures known in the colonies as the Intolerable Acts, including the Boston Port Bill, which shut off the city's sea trade pending payment for the destroyed tea. The British government's efforts to single out Massachusetts for punishment served only to unite the colonies and impel the drift toward war.[48]

When I read the history of the Boston Tea Party, it evoked things in my mind:

- ❖ protest
- ❖ tyranny
- ❖ governmental overreach
- ❖ greed
- ❖ non-compliance
- ❖ corruption
- ❖ control
- ❖ civil disobedience
- ❖ the people
- ❖ freedom
- ❖ liberty
- ❖ unity

---

[48] Britannica. (2023) *Boston Tea Party*

❖ war

I pondered that thought again: There really is *nothing new under the sun*.

In the words of Samuel Adams, labelled a *radical* by the powerful elites of the day, *"It is no dishonour to be in a minority in the cause of liberty and virtue."*

The year is now 2023, and we have collectively just come through a period of history where all those words also apply.

It *always* appears to be the minority, the small *remnant*, as the Bible calls it (Romans 11:5), who are the ones that stand up to tyrannical leadership, corruption, and evil.

It is this minority group that is perceived to be radical and a nuisance by authority and the mass population—these people who are disrupting the status quo and causing conflict and disharmony between power and the people.

But it is often this same group who bring about the change that is needed, abolish the evil, and bring light and justice into corrupt situations in this world.

I, too, have been honoured to be part of this *"radical"* group of people in the cause of liberty and freedom, and I can resonate with Samuel Adams and his team of disobedient civilians.

Somebody once said ,*"The only thing necessary for the triumph of evil is for good men to do nothing,"* and that is true.

The phrase warns against complacency and inaction against evil, as it allows it to continue or proliferate.

Scripture speaks about the minority overcoming evil (even when the odds were stacked against them) and the remnant army of believers who will be raised up to fight the satanic powers and principalities of darkness in the last days.

The prophet Elijah, defeating the prophets of Baal, said:

"Yet I will leave seven thousand in Israel, all the knees that have not bowed to Baal and every mouth that has not kissed him." **1 Kings 19:18**

And then there was the story of Gideon's 300 chosen men who defeated the Midianite army:

So he (Gideon) brought the people down to the water. And the Lord said to Gideon, "You shall separate everyone who laps the water with his tongue as a dog laps, as well as everyone who kneels to drink." Now, the number of those who lapped, putting their hand to their mouth, was 300 men; but all the rest of the people kneeled to drink water. The Lord said to Gideon, "I will deliver you with the 300 men who lapped and will give the Midianites into your hands; so let all the other people go, each man to his home." **Judges 7:5-7**

The faithful remnant of believers is described in the Bible as blessed beyond measure despite their failures and weaknesses:

Now on that day the remnant of Israel, and those of the house of Jacob who have escaped, will no longer rely on the one who struck them, but will truly rely on the Lord, the Holy One of Israel. A remnant will return, the remnant of Jacob, to the mighty God. For though your people, Israel, may be like the sand of the sea, only a remnant within them will return; A destruction is determined, overflowing with righteousness. **Isaiah 10:20-22**

God will often use the *small* things in this world—the seemingly insignificant, the overlooked, the underdog, the lowly, the despised, the tiny minority—to bring down to nothing those of great status and power, in worldly human terms, and bring forth His kingdom purposes, righteousness, and justice:

> *And the base things of the world and the despised*
> *God has chosen, the things that are not, so that He*
> *may nullify the things that are.* **1 Corinthians 1:28**

We went out for a late lunch shortly before taking our transfer to the airport for the flight home. A woman was sitting across the restaurant with a t-shirt on with the slogan "In God we trust. Everyone else, bring data." My husband said he felt the Holy Spirit tell him that I should speak to her.

Being British, I hadn't realised that this was the campaign strapline for Mike Bloomberg when he ran for the 2020 presidential campaign for the Democrats.

Who knew?

This woman was clearly a keen follower and still donning the merchandise.

We started chatting at length, and she was interested in our travel plans and where we had been and what we had seen over the past three weeks.

When I told her about Plymouth Rock, she exclaimed, "You must go and visit Leiden next for the final piece of the jigsaw!"

"Where is Leiden?" I replied, feeling slightly ignorant.

"It's in The Netherlands," she replied.

I felt goosebumps on my arms.

We had flown out to the United States via Amsterdam and were going back the same way. Originally, we had a very short layover between our flights, but a couple of weeks before departure, the airline had emailed me to say that our flight had been cancelled, and we now had an eight-hour layover instead.

I had felt highly frustrated at the time, but now, I was beginning to wonder, *Is this another divine appointment—another God wink?*

The Lord Himself goes before us, and He directs our path.

> *"And the Lord is the one who is going ahead*
> *of you."* **Deuteronomy 31:8**

She went onto explain that her ancestor was William Brewster.

In a quiet English village named Scrooby, a group of believers met to observe the Lord's Day. There were no choirs, no bells, no incense, and none of the ordinary trappings of ceremonial worship. Few would have guessed that this small group of believers in an obscure English village would become the Pilgrim fathers, and that the candle that burned here in this manor home would one day "light a thousand."

The owner of the home in which the believers of Scrooby met was a gentleman named William Brewster. Unlike many of his fellow Separatists, Brewster had been born into the landed gentry. He had studied at Cambridge and had been in the service of the English ambassador to the Netherlands, where he was exposed to the Reformed Faith.

When Brewster returned to England after his time in the Netherlands, he began to take an active role in the leadership of the Separatist church. William and his wife, Mary, desired to worship the Lord in a simple way without the man-made trappings of ceremonial formalism. Following the campaign led by Archbishop Bancroft to force Puritan ministers out of the church, the Brewsters invited John Robinson and Richard Clifton (who were both early Separatists) to meet in their manor house in Scrooby for worship services on the Lord's Day. This was a courageous step for an English gentleman.

William Brewster held the official position of Postmaster in Scrooby. His large manor house had ample room for the 40 or 50 believers who would assemble there each Lord's Day. During these days in Scrooby, William and Mary Brewster extended an offer of hospitality to a young-orphaned teenager named William Bradford, who often walked to Scrooby and stayed in their manor house on Saturdays so that he could attend the worship services on the Lord's Day.

When restrictions and political pressure began to threaten the Scrooby group, the need to find a refuge elsewhere became apparent. It was William Brewster who, with his political and diplomatic experience, organized the removal of the Scrooby congregation to the Netherlands in 1608.

The congregation lived in Amsterdam for a year, however, contention among the other Separatists convinced Robinson and Brewster to lead their congregation to the city of Leiden. William Brewster made a living in Leiden by teaching English to Dutch university students. His wisdom and experience soon gave him the trusted position of elder in the congregation.

In addition to his duties as an English teacher and an elder in the church, William Brewster took up the task of operating a small printing press in Leiden. Brewster was able to print and distribute pamphlets in Leiden which were illegal to print in England. He printed a controversial pamphlet written by the Scottish minister David Calderwood which criticized the legitimacy of the 1618 Perth Assembly and attacked the innovations imposed by the Five Articles of Perth. The pamphlet argued against the Romish ceremonies of the Church of England and defended the simple worship of God against man-made innovations. When the outraged king found out about the publication, he ordered an international manhunt for both the author and the printer. Leiden University offered their protection to William Brewster, and he was able to evade arrest.

In the midst of increasing political pressure, a church torn by division and schism, and a worldly and licentious Dutch society, William Brewster and the other leaders of the congregation believed that it would be best for their children if they would leave the Netherlands and seek a home in the wilderness of the New World.

Brewster's wisdom and experience became a stabilizing influence during the voyage and during the difficult early days in Plymouth. Without the pastoral care of John Robinson, William Brewster became the spiritual leader of the congregation and was the man who was often called upon to preach the Bible and lead the singing of Psalms each Lord's Day.

For his services to the colony, William Brewster was granted land among the islands of Boston Harbor. Four of these islands still bear his name to this day: Great Brewster, Little Brewster, Middle Brewster, and Outer Brewster.

William Brewster went to be with the Lord on April 18, 1644. He was buried on Burial Hill in Plymouth, overlooking the harbour where the Mayflower took anchor in the New World. His memorial stone is inscribed with these words, "Elder William Brewster, Patriarch of the Pilgrims and their Ruling Elder."[49]

Aboard Flight DL258, Boston Logan International to Amsterdam Schiphol Airport

I smiled at the similarities between what William Brewster encountered in the early 1600s and what many Christians had recently journeyed through over 400 years later:

❖ Parts of the Church leaving the confines of an established church building and gathering in smaller numbers in people's homes for Spirit-filled worship and biblically based teaching

❖ The simplicity of the Christian faith; following the teachings of Jesus Christ; losing the religiosity and ceremonial man-made additions

❖ When restrictions and political pressure began to threaten gatherings of worship, believers would naturally seek refuge elsewhere

---

[49] Discerning History. (2021) *William Brewster: Patriarch of the Pilgrims*

- ❖ The writing and sharing of truth and biblically-based literature, used in rebellion against the propaganda and unsound teaching from authority

- ❖ Wisdom when to stay in a place and when to move under the advancement of tyranny, persecution, and segregation

- ❖ The pursuing of liberty, freedom, and truth

During the lockdowns of 2020 and 2021, many small gatherings took place in homes, under canvas, and in woodland areas when the churches followed governmental recommendation to close their doors to the people.

Many of us sought God's Word in its pure and raw state and asked the Lord for divine revelation—no interpretations, no commentaries, no opinions of man. It was refreshing to lose all the distractions of what church had been and the "show" and extravagance of what it had become. We kept it simple.

When worship gatherings were shut down, I recall gathering outside in the local park. We were socially distanced; yet, people would still call the police to report us.

We just made alterative arrangements and sought refuge elsewhere.

No man was going to stop us from worshipping the God of the angel armies and exercising our right to worship, which is, of course, a fundamental human right.

Many biblical tracts were published speaking out against the incoming tyranny and deception. These were given out at organised freedom protests to thousands of spiritually searching individuals who had tasted evil and were in search of God.

Monthly newspapers were written sharing the truth about what was really going on in the world behind the mainstream media smoke screen;

facts and data were shared all over social media, and a family of like-minded people from all across the world were brought together.

I knew of friends and whole family units who moved towns, counties, even countries to escape the tyranny, spiritual persecution, and avoid having to take a mandated experimental medication in order to simply keep their job, have access to basic healthcare, or to send their child to school. In the United Kingdom, had it not been for the NHS100k (a resistance movement of healthcare activists), the U.K. government would have mandated the injections for nurses and midwives, which could have then led to a more extensive unethical mandate for university students and schoolchildren, which we saw in other countries across the commonwealth.

During that time, there were many new contacts, old friends, and medical colleagues struggling with what to do and feeling trapped by their employers. As a former midwife, I was able to help them with their plight and speak up on their behalf, writing numerous letters, attending protests, sourcing alternative solutions where possible, and signing scores of petitions.

We prayed a lot and for many.

Some people now say it felt like we were at war.

That's because we were.

A silent biological and psychological war—the aftermath of which will most likely be felt for many generations to come.

Leiden is located on the Oude Rijn, twenty-five miles south of Amsterdam.

There is a direct train that goes there from the airport.

I knew God wanted us to go there the following day.

CHAPTER FIFTEEN

The great hope, and for the propagating and advancing the gospel of the kingdom of Christ in those remote parts of the world.
William Bradford[50]

Leiden, the Netherlands

Leiden is like a small version of Amsterdam.

There are still lots of bicycles to avoid and canals to negotiate, but the undeniable aroma of hemp on the streets is far less noticeable.

The people are friendly, speak impeccable English, but made me feel rather short.

We walked from the train station to the *Pieterskerk*, a late-Gothic Dutch Protestant church, where the pastor John Robinson was buried and the Pilgrim Fathers had gathered to worship.

There was nobody around.

No tourists.

Just a peace, an ethereal silence, and a grace that filled the pause.

Standing in Pieterskerkhof felt like a beautiful end to an enlightening journey.

---

[50] William Bradford, Plymrock.org *online*

We took the train back to Amsterdam and walked across the bridge toward *Herengracht*, strolling hand-in-hand over the picturesque bridges, admiring the colourful tulips and the quirky canal houses, and enjoying the smell of baking from the many *Koffiehuezen*, the warm summer breeze gently brushing our tired faces as we tried to beat the jet lag and stay awake for the transit home.

Coming back to the Netherlands after that whole encounter felt like my spiritual life had gone full circle. I found Jesus because of an evangelist who had courageously pioneered a ministry in the Red Light District of Amsterdam, and here I was again, thirty years later, seeking the same Lord for direction for the next chapter of my calling as an evangelist of the gospel.

It felt like a rebirth moment.

A new beginning.

Not the end, but in fact, the start of a new and exciting adventure with God!

CHAPTER SIXTEEN

Strength and dignity are her clothing,
And she smiles at the future.
Proverbs 31:25

Harrogate, North Yorkshire

Throughout biblical history, God has been passionately pursing His people.

He has given them guidelines and commandments for godly and ful-filled living, but He allows them the free will to make their own choices.

When they get things wrong and they truly repent for their error, He forgives them, and He promises to heal their land:

> *And My people who are called by My name humble*
> *themselves, and pray and seek My face, and turn from*
> *their wicked ways, then I will hear from heaven, and I will*
> *forgive their sin and will heal their land.* **2 Chronicles 7:14**

I truly believe we are at a crucial 2 Chronicles 7:14 moment in history.

Those reading this who are in church leadership and part of the Body of Christ need to humble themselves before God and repent (or turn away) from all wickedness and ungodly decisions, repent of any collaboration with the evil world systems, and repent where they have knowingly or naively been deceived.

The Bride of Christ, the Church, needs to set itself apart from the world, rise up and be counted in this spiritual war against the dominions of darkness.

We are living at a significant point in human history.

The Bible tells us that things are going to get tough for Christians, and many of us have felt the squeeze of that over the past few years.

But we also have that *blessed hope*; that glorious hope that the world does not have.

We eagerly await the return of our King Jesus and the restoration of all things.

For the eagerly awaiting creation waits for the revealing of the sons and daughters of God. For the creation was subjected to futility, not willingly, but because of Him who subjected it, in hope that the creation itself also will be set free from its slavery to corruption into the freedom of the glory of the children of God. For we know that the whole creation groans and suffers the pains of childbirth together until now. And not only that, but also we ourselves, having the first fruits of the Spirit, even we ourselves groan within ourselves, waiting eagerly for our adoption as sons and daughters, the redemption of our body. For in hope we have been saved, but hope that is seen is not hope; for who hopes for what he already sees? But if we hope for what we do not see, through perseverance we wait eagerly for it. **Romans 8:19-25**

Creation groans and suffers the pains of childbirth together until now.

I'm a trained midwife; I've had three children of my own—I know a lot about birth pains. It's a perfect analogy of where we are at.

Contractions of the uterus during a woman's labour do four specific things:

- ❖ they get closer together;
- ❖ they get more and more regular;
- ❖ they get longer in duration; and
- ❖ they *certainly* get increasingly painful.

This is right up until the baby is born, and then, the pain is forgotten, replaced with joy.

> *Whenever a woman is in labour she has pain, because*
> *her hour has come; but when she gives birth to the*
> *child, she no longer remembers the anguish because*
> *of the joy that a child has been born into the world.*
> *Therefore you too have grief now; but I will see you*
> *again, and your heart will rejoice, and no one is going*
> *to take your joy away from you.* **John 16:21-22**

Jesus also told us there would be birth pains in the signs of His return (Matthew 24). Whilst speaking to His disciples, He lists many signs of His return: wars, rumours of wars, nations rising up against other nations, kingdoms against kingdoms—perhaps that's the kingdom of God, rising up against the kingdom of darkness in spiritual warfare.

Have you felt the battle too?

Famines and earthquakes.

Jesus says these are the *beginning* of birth pains.

But as these things on our watch seem to be speeding up and the pain and the suffering increasing—the light is getting brighter.

God is doing His own "Great Reset."

God's Great Reset.

Our *blessed hope*, the appearing of our great God and Saviour Jesus Christ on that *great and dreadful day* (Malachi 4:5).

As believers in Christ, we have this sure and steadfast anchor of the soul – a hope that enters into the inner place behind the curtain, where Jesus has gone as a forerunner on our behalf.

And so, we must not live in fear.

We have been set free from sin and a spirit of slavery!

We must have our minds set on the Spirit which leads to life and peace.

We have received the spirit of adoption, and we are children of God.

That is our identity.

Our *only* identity.

We must recognise that suffering and persecution are part of the deal for those that take the narrow path seriously and live an authentic life for God.

The broad path, the things of this world which are temporal, lead to destruction, which will ultimately only lead to death.

Peter said:

> *If you are insulted for the name of Christ, you
> are blessed, because the Spirit of glory, and
> of God, rests upon you.* **1 Peter 4:14**

And Paul said:

> *And not only this, but we also celebrate in our tribulations,
> knowing that tribulation brings about perseverance; and
> perseverance, proven character; and proven character,
> hope; and hope does not disappoint, because the love*

of God has been poured out within our hearts through
the Holy Spirit who was given to us. **Romans 5:3-5**

God, in His kindness and infinite love, has taught me so many things during the times of trial, persecution, hardship, and pain. It is in these sacred moments that He teaches us, challenges us, breaks us, and refines us into becoming the person that He has created us to be.

The past few years have truly deepened my relationship with the Lord as I have solely trusted in Him and He has entrusted me.

- ❖ When He speaks, I listen.
- ❖ When He gives a watchman warning, I take heed.
- ❖ When He reveals something to me, I take note.
- ❖ When He convicts me, I repent.
- ❖ When He guides me, I follow.
- ❖ When He tells me, I obey.

And when He calls me, I will go.

As Christians, we, and the whole of creation, inwardly groan for the return of King Jesus as depicted in the Book of Revelation; we will be finally set free from the slavery and deception of this dark and corrupt world, knowing that when Christ appears on the clouds, then we also will appear with Him in glory.

Be alert.

Keep watch.

Stay awake.

But where is this fallen, broken, and hopeless world heading?

What new evil is coming down the track?

Humbly I realise that the Lord chose me and appointed me as a watchman during this extraordinary time in world history. Why me, I do not know, but *what He told me in the darkness, I told in the light; and what He whispered in my ear, I proclaimed on the housetops* (Matthew 10:27).

And with many other courageous and defiant people, I went on the frontline of this biological and psychological *war* for the next three years.

I never once pushed my own view, for what does that even matter? I simply shared a different narrative (with links to clinical data and scientific evidence) which happened to be contrary to public opinion and groupthink at the time.

For the Book of Ezekiel says this:

> Now the word of the Lord came to me, saying, "Son of man, speak to the sons of your people and say to them, 'If I bring a sword upon a land, and the people of the land take one man from among them and make him their watchman, and he sees the sword coming upon the land and blows the horn and warns the people, then someone who hears the sound of the horn but does not take warning, and a sword comes and takes him away, his blood will be on his own head. He heard the sound of the horn but did not take warning; his blood will be on himself. But had he taken warning, he would have saved his life. **But if the watchman sees the sword coming and does not blow the horn and the people are not warned, and a sword comes and takes a person from them, he is taken away for his wrongdoing; but I will require his blood from the watchman's hand.'" Ezekiel 33:1-6**

If the Lord has commissioned you to be a *watchman on the walls*, and you have a healthy fear of Him, then you have no choice but to speak up.

It has been a privilege being the leaders of a thriving ministry in our hometown over the past season, not a role we take lightly, and my husband and I continually ask the Lord to keep us humble in that walk.

But it has also been challenging and out of our comfort zones, and we have had to make ourselves vulnerable speaking up about such important issues, feeling at many a time that we were the small fish swimming upstream against the tide.

When the Lord gives you something that you must say, you shouldn't hesitate to do so, but there were many occasions I remember praying out loud to Him; something like Jesus did in the Garden of Gethsemane:

> *"Father, if you are willing, remove this cup from Me,*
> *yet not my will, but Yours be done."* **Luke 22:42**

It was just too hard at times.

Too painful.

Some people simply couldn't hear it, and so, they left and never came back.

And if you have an evangelistic and pastoral heart, that really, really hurts.

Am I even being loving, Lord?

The daily personal challenges and reckoning with God were real.

I probably went through that process on a daily basis with every post I shared on social media; I wrestled with it every time I had the courage to speak into that void of silence and pain that so many people were struggling with.

That golden calf that could not be mentioned.

We started to offer prayers for healing of the sick for those who had been injured after taking the "safe and effective" product, a substance that was unethically pushed on the population with questionable trial data and unethical methods of advertising and promotion.

It was a courageous move, but we knew the Lord wanted us to do it.

We blew the trumpet, and we started to get noticed locally, nationally and internationally online, and more and more people started to come along to Harrogate Filling Station to receive prayers for healing where they had been damaged so unnecessarily and their stories were not being listened to elsewhere.

The ministry became a place of refuge and healing.

It became a sanctuary for many who felt abandoned by their churches. They felt safe.

The people were traumatised too from what they had lived through, broken in body, mind and spirit and many with depression and PTSD, anxiety and fear from what they had seen, heard, and experienced firsthand.

Healing prayers then began to include prayers of deliverance from various demonic spirits that were gripping people from living the lives that God wanted them to have; entry points had been opened during that dark and oppressive time, either unknowingly or by choice, and they needed to be set free.

The words of Isaiah 61:1-3 began to feel timely and relevant for us:

> *The Spirit of the Lord GOD is upon me, Because the
> LORD has anointed me To **bring good news to the
> afflicted**; He has sent me **to bind up the brokenhearted**,
> To **proclaim liberty** to captives and **freedom to
> prisoners**; To proclaim the favourable year of the LORD
> And the day of vengeance of our God; To comfort
> all who mourn. To grant those who mourn in Zion,*
>
> *Giving them a garland instead of ashes,
> The oil of gladness instead of mourning,
> The mantle of praise instead of a spirit of fainting.
> So they will be called oaks of righteousness,*

The planting of the LORD, that He may be glorified.

We also started to hold healing prayer appointments online for those that had been injured and were suffering and lived too far away to travel–some, too, who lived internationally–and we were seeing the Lord heal them in wonderful ways. Miraculous healings were happening instantly and within days and weeks of having prayer.

Many of these people had previously been to the medics and healthcare providers, and they couldn't help them or join the dots about their story.

They would come to us, and we would listen and pray into their situations.

Many had found faith in Jesus Christ only recently. Some were being saved and healed all at once; burdens were being lifted off, and faith was being restored.

The Lord was pouring out His Spirit upon us and turning hopeless situations into new life and spirits of despair into garments of praise. God was *giving them a garland instead of ashes and the oil of gladness instead of mourning* (Isaiah 61:3).

It was beautiful thing to see and be a part of.

Now the Lord is the Spirit, and where the Spirit of the Lord is, there is freedom. **2 Corinthians 3:17**

Only Jesus.

As I type, praying for the sick and those traumatised because of the past few years is still happening on almost a daily basis.

I don't know when the suffering and repercussions from that will ever end.

Perhaps it will remain for generations and generations to come.

Or maybe the Lord Jesus is coming back very soon.

But three things I do know.

I know that the Lord is still seated on the throne:

God reigns over the nations, God sits
on His holy throne. **Isaiah 61:3**

I know that He is above all things:

He who comes from above is above all; the one who is
only from the earth is of the earth and speaks of the earth.
He who comes from heaven is above all. **John 3:31**

I know that the victory has already been won by Jesus on the cross:

He said, "It is finished!" And He bowed His
head and gave up His spirit. **John 19:30**

I do not want to speculate in this book what might be yet to come, but I truly believe that the enemy has overplayed his hand.

I am hopeful that more people will become aware of the extent of evil in the world. The madness and depravity in society is so obvious and blatant that it has awoken many of those who were in previous slumber.

I believe the ultimate goal is totalitarian overreach by the few over the majority, achieved by whatever means. This includes world domination, governance and control of the human race through mandated healthcare schemes, surveillance cameras, digital identification, transhumanism, social credit systems, climate lockdowns, smart cities, central banking digital currency (often referred to as CBDC), and other demonically inspired solutions.

More propaganda.

More health crises.

More fearmongering.

Collectively, our faith and spiritual wellbeing are being attacked, and speaking up for truth, standing on God's unchanging Word, and defending even the fundamentals of what it means to be a Christian is becoming more problematic every day. Sadly, the attacks are coming from the Church itself, as well as the world and its satanically influenced culture.

Alas, we hold joys and sorrow together.

Jesus once said:

> *Truly, truly I say to you that you will weep and*
> *mourn, but the world will rejoice; you will grieve, but*
> *your grief will be turned into joy!* **John 16:20**

The battle will get harder, but the harvest of souls is getting bigger.

In the meantime, there is a glorious gospel to preach, people to be healed, and lives to be set free in the name of Jesus Christ.

CHAPTER SEVENTEEN

*Baruch Haba B'shem Adonai – Blessed is the one
who comes in the name of the Lord.*
Psalm 118:26

Jersualem, Israel

It had been an exhilarating spiritual trip from start to finish.

Starting at Mount Carmel in the north of the country, visiting Lake Galilee, Capernaum (the city of *comfort*), and walking in the footsteps of Jesus, before working our way down south, past Nazareth to Jerusalem, for the final part of the tour. The Lord blessed us as we travelled, and Bible stories came alive at every marker.

On the penultimate day, we visited the Temple Mount, and I stood barefoot on the remains of Jerusalem's main street, which was still paved with flagstones and edged with curbstones, running along the length of the Western Wall.

A place of peace.

A place of spiritual energy and significance.

Like so many supernatural experiences in my life, it wasn't so much how it looked that day that I can remember—it was how I felt.

A divine encounter.

I sat down on one of the collapsed stones and tried to take it all in.

One of the stones (a replica) bore a Hebrew inscription:

"to the place of trumpeting to..."

It was likely to have marked the place at the top of the southwest corner of the Temple Mount, where the trumpeter would have made important announcements such as the inauguration and the close of the Sabbath.

The watchman on the walls of Jerusalem.

I smiled.

In the same way, I can remember how that olive tree felt as I held tightly onto it and poured out my heart to God in the garden, tears rolling down my face.

The peace. Shalom.

The Garden of Gethsemane (which means *"oil press"* in Aramaic).

> *Then Jesus came with them to a place called Gethsemane, and told His disciples, "Sit here while I go over there and pray." And He took Peter and the two sons of Zebedee with Him, and began to be grieved and distressed. Then He said to them, "My soul is deeply grieved, to the point of death; remain here and keep watch with Me."* **Matthew 26:36-38**

This was the place where Jesus Himself was crushed, broken, wrestling with His Father before His arrest and crucifixion, sweating tears of blood and pleading to take the cup of suffering away from Him.

> *And He went a little beyond them, and fell on His face and prayed, saying, "My Father, if it is possible, let this cup pass from Me; yet not as I will, but as You will."* **Matthew 26:39**

Jesus knew what it was like to be given a mandate from God that He didn't want to do, but He remained obedient until the very end.

I now could understand that too.

God had got me, and He would never let me go.

The Lord is always trying to teach us, refine us, and prepare us for our future.

He births new giftings within us and helps them come to fruition. He takes things away to keep us humble and dependent on His love.

It's the way of discipleship. It's the way of the cross.

God is constantly speaking to us, if only we would listen, and He is constantly showing us, if only we would notice.

It's worth repeating what He demands of you and me:

- ❖ How much are you willing to lose for this?
- ❖ How long are you willing to wait?
- ❖ Will you trust Me?

CHAPTER EIGHTEEN

This gospel of the kingdom shall be preached in the whole world as a testimony to all the nations, and then the end will come.
Matthew 24:14

The Nations, the World

There is no better job than being an ambassador of the Good News, an evangelist to the nations, and ministering in signs and wonders.

My love for sharing this message of hope, salvation, and deliverance for *all* of God's people burns like a roaring fire inside of my heart—not just for the Gentiles (those born of non-Jewish descent) to know Christ, but for the Jewish people to recognise Yeshua (Jesus) as their risen Messiah.

Because of my Hebraic roots, it excites me that not only are we seeing the restoration of people to the land of Israel, but we are also seeing the restoration of the gospel of the kingdom to the people of Israel, the messianic Jewish remnant, on our watch.

Bible prophesy is being fulfilled.

These are the days of awakening.

I believe we are at a *kairos* moment in history—a propitious moment for action.

The enemy may have been advancing his plans and assembled his satanic army, but God is using the adversary to turn many hearts back to him. He is raising up His humble servants—men and women of God *who have clean hands and a pure heart* (Psalm 24:4) and a hunger and pursuit for justice and righteousness—to join in the fight and advance His kingdom here on Earth.

These are fully yielded disciples of the Lord Jesus Christ who are equipped and ready to take up the mandate which Jesus gave in Matthew 10:7-8:

> *"And as you go, preach, saying, 'The kingdom of heaven has come near.' Heal the sick, raise the dead, cleanse those with leprosy, cast out demons."*

The consequences of the unethical and tyrannical lockdowns and other detrimental repercussions of the last few years have given a significant rise in poor mental wellbeing, health issues, relationship breakdowns, loss of livelihood, and financial devastation to so many families.

Coupled with the silencing of churches and oppression of spiritual life, there has also been a door opened to the occult and witchcraft, and the powers of darkness have been given an opportunistic platform to infiltrate society on a grand scale.

As a ministry, we have noticed a continued demand for people seeking healing prayer for infirmity and disease and deliverance from evil spirits, often travelling a long distance to attend those appointments or visit a meeting. As time goes on, we continue to expect an increase in this type of ministry, as God is pouring out His Spirit and anointing in this hour and setting the captives free.

It is no longer an option to be merely a spectator in this spiritual war.

The Lord is calling each and every one of His followers, His remnant army, to put on the spiritual armour and take up this final hour mandate.

The kingdom of Heaven is near.

For over thirty years I have been an evangelist who loves Jesus and who uses her voice to share the Good News of the gospel. When the Lord first prompted me to write this book, He reminded me of a much-loved worship song which was popular around the time of my full immersion baptism in the early 1990s.

He asked me to exchange my voice for a pen.

I strongly believe that the verses of "I hear the Sound of Rustling" (Ronnie Wilson, 1979) are a prophetic clarion call for such a time as this. Will you listen and take the charge?

"I hear the sound of rustling in the leaves of the trees,
the Spirit of the Lord has come down on the earth."
Come, Holy Spirit!

"The church that seemed in slumber has now risen from its knees,
and dry bones are responding with the fruits of new birth."
Wake up, Church!

"Oh, this is now a time for declaration,
the word will go to all men everywhere."
Preach the gospel!

"The church is here for healing of the nations,
behold the day of Jesus drawing near."
Heal the sick!

"My tongue will be the pen of a ready writer,
and what the Father gives to me I'll sing;
I only want to be His breath,
I only want to glorify the King.

And all around the world the body waits expectantly,
the promise of the Father is now ready to fall."
The time is now. Can you see it?

"The watchmen on the tower all exhort us to prepare,
and the church responds—a people who will answer the call."
Are you listening? Will you go?

"And this is not a phase which is passing;
it's the start of an age that is to come."
The Spirit is here. Can you feel it?

"And where is the wise man and the scoffer?
Before the face of Jesus they are dumb."
Will you speak the truth in love? Will you lose the fear of man?

"My tongue will be the pen of a ready writer,
and what the father gives to me I'll sing;
I only want to be His breath,
I only want to glorify the King.

A body now prepared by God and ready for war,
the prompting of the Spirit is our word of command."
Are you battle ready?

"We rise, a mighty army, at the bidding of the Lord,
the devils see and fear, for their time is at hand."
If God is for us, who can be against us?

"And children of the Lord hear our commission
that we should love and serve our God as one."

For where there is unity, the Lord will command a blessing!

*"The Spirit won't be hindered by division
in the perfect work that Jesus has begun."*
Amen!

*Lord, I trust You. I am fully surrendered to Your
direction and Your calling over my life, wherever
that may lead, wherever You would have me go.*

"Here am I. Send me!" **Isaiah 6:8**

In the Book of Hebrews, it says:

*But we are not among those who shrink back to
destruction, but of those who have faith for the
safekeeping of the soul.* **Hebrews 10:39**

This is a mandate to the whole Church of Jesus Christ.

We must not *shrink back* from the task set before us but move valiantly against the evil that has been unleashed upon our broken and confused world.

We must not *look back*, like the Israelite slaves did upon Egypt, longing with heavy hearts for what has been and yearning for the counterfeit comforts and illusions which may have made us feel safe and secure before.

Instead, it is time to *fight* back and to *press on toward the goal for the prize of the upward call of God in Christ Jesus* (Philippians 3:14).

It is time to march on and look forward toward the Promised Land.

I have found the following powerful Bible scriptures challenging, affirming, and formational in my personal pilgrimage as an evangelist.

I hope they bless and encourage you too.

*But as for you, use self-restraint in all things,
endure hardship, do the work of an evangelist,
fulfil your ministry.* **2 Timothy 4:5**

*But sanctify Christ as Lord in your hearts, always
being ready to make a defense to everyone who
asks you to give an account for the hope that is in
you, but with gentleness and respect.* **1 Peter 3:15**

*Jesus answered, "I am the way and the truth and the life. No
one comes to the Father except through me."* **John 14:6**

*Then He said to His disciples, "The harvest is plentiful, but the
workers are few. Therefore, plead with the Lord of the harvest
to send out workers into His harvest."* **Matthew 9:37-38**

*"Go, therefore, and make disciples of all the nations,
baptizing them in the name of the Father and the
Son and the Holy Spirit, teaching them to follow all
that I commanded you; and behold, I am with you
always, to the end of the age."* **Matthew 28:19-20**

If you would like to re-dedicate your commitment to upholding and proclaiming the gospel of Jesus Christ, you can affirm that promise by joining in the words of the Pilgrim's Prayer of 1607:

THE PILGRIM'S PRAYER OF 1607

*"We do hereby dedicate this Land, and ourselves, to reach
the People within these shores with the Gospel of Jesus Christ,
and to raise up Godly generations after us, and with these*

generations take the Kingdom of God to all the earth. May this Covenant of Dedication remain to all generations, as long as this earth remains and may this land, along with England, be evangelists to the world.

May all who see this cross remember what we have done here, and may those who come here to inhabit join us in this Covenant and this most noble work, that the Holy Scriptures may be fulfilled. From these very shores the gospel shall go forth, not only to this new world, but the entire world."

If you would like to say sorry to God for anything you've done wrong and would like to invite Jesus Christ into your heart today, you can say this prayer now:

THE SALVATION PRAYER

Lord Jesus,
Thank you for loving me; thank you for saving me.
Thank you that You died on a cross so that I could go free.
Thank you that You rose again so I could have eternal life.
Lord Jesus, I confess my sins and ask for Your forgiveness.
Please come into my heart right now as my Lord, my God, and my Saviour.
Take complete control of my life; help me to walk in Your footsteps daily.
By the power of the Holy Spirit,

AMEN

Mayflower II, Plymouth, MA.

Plymouth Rock, Plymouth, MA.

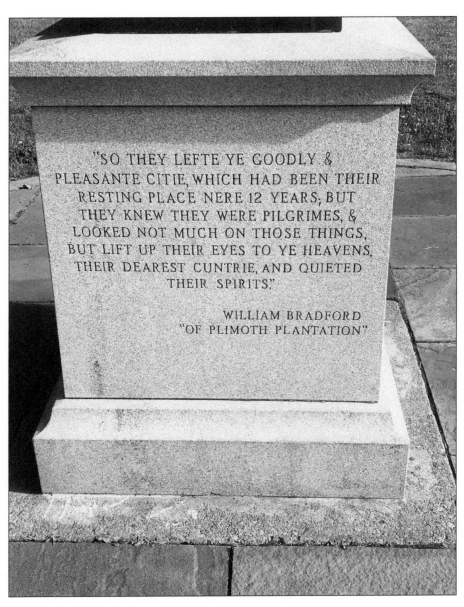

"SO THEY LEFTE YE GOODLY &
PLEASANTE CITIE, WHICH HAD BEEN THEIR
RESTING PLACE NERE 12 YEARS; BUT
THEY KNEW THEY WERE PILGRIMES, &
LOOKED NOT MUCH ON THOSE THINGS,
BUT LIFT UP THEIR EYES TO YE HEAVENS,
THEIR DEAREST CUNTRIE, AND QUIETED
THEIR SPIRITS."

WILLIAM BRADFORD
"OF PLIMOTH PLANTATION"

William Bradford Statue, Plymouth, MA.

Wesleyan Grove, Martha's Vineyard, MA.

A quiet time with Jesus, Cape Cod, MA.

Cliff Walk, Newport, RI.

Atlantic Ocean, Newport, RI.

St Mary's Parish, Newport, RI.

Long Beach, Long Island, NY.

Central Park, New York City, NY.

View from the Empire State Building, New York City, NY.

Statue of Liberty, New York City, NY.

"Short Term Disruption" sign from God.

Lighthouse Way, New York City, NY.

Outside Ronald Reagan Building, Washington, D.C.

Lincoln Memorial, Washington, D.C.

"Spirit of Pan," Caesarea Philippi, Israel.

Colonial Williamsburg, VA.

Bruton Parish Church, VA.

Wintergreen Resort, VA.

Memorial Cross, Cape Henry, VA.

Hope at Memorial Cross, Cape Henry, VA.

Boston, MA.

Boston Tea Party, Boston, MA.

Joy Street, Boston, MA.

Pieterskirk, Leiden, the Netherlands.

Pieterskirk, Leiden, the Netherlands.

Jerusalem, Israel.

Garden of Gethsemane, Jerusalem, Israel.

The Filling Station, Harrogate, UK.

BIBLIOGRAPHY

Smithsonian (2023) *George Santayana, The Life of Reason, 1905*

www.si.edu/object/saam_1984.124.194 (Accessed 20 September 2023)

NASB Super Giant Print Bible (1995) *Holy Bible*. USA, Zondervan

Introduction

Lions Gates Entertainment (2023) *Jesus Revolution*. www.jesusrevolution.movie (Accessed 13 July 2023)

Lyrics STANDS4 LLC. (2023) *"You Said" Hillsong Music/ Reuben Morley*. www.lyrics.com/lyric/5473705/Hillsong/You+Said (Accessed 22 August 2023)

Chapter 2

Metaxas, Eric. (2022) *Letter to the American Church*. USA, Salem Books.

William Bradford, *Of Plymouth Plantation* (New York: Alfred A Knopf, 2002), 52.

Chapter 3

Dartmouth Mayflower (2023) *Dartmouth Mayflower: at the helm of history*. www.dartmouthmayflower400.uk/ (Accessed 17 July 2023)

American Ancestors (2017) *Trouble with Speedwell*. www.vitabrevis.americanancestors.org/2017/12/trouble-with-speedwell (Accessed 13 September 2023)

A&E Television Networks (2023) *History.* www.history.com/topics/colonial-america/mayflower (Accessed 17 July 2023)

Lutzer, Erwin W. (2022) *No Reason to Hide.* Oregon, Harvest House Publishers.

Cambridge Dictionary (2023) *Pilgrim.* www.dictionary.cambridge.org (Accessed 17 July 2023)

Chapter 4

McClung, Floyd. (1985) *Father Heart of God.* USA, David C. Cook

New York State Museum. (2023) *Martin Luther King Jr.,"Speech to commemorate the centennial of the Preliminary Emancipation Proclamation",* Park Sheraton Hotel, New York City, September 12th, 1962. www.nysm.nysed.gov (Accessed 14 September 2023).

Chapter 5

Good Reads (2023). *John Wesley.* www.goodreads.com/quotes (Accessed 22 July 2023)

Wikipedia (2023) *Wesleyan Grove.* www.en.wikipedia.org/wiki/Wesleyan_Grove (Accessed 19 July 2023)

Britannica (2023) *John Wesley: English Clergyman.* www.britannica.com/biography/John-Wesley (Accessed 19 July 2023)

Martha's Vineyard Camp Meeting Association (2023) www.mvcma.org (Accessed 20 July 2023)

Universal Pictures (1975) Steven Spielberg, John Williams. *JAWS.* USA.

Chapter 6

Cape Cod Chamber of Commerce (2023) *Convention and Visitors Bureau.* www.capecodchamber.org (Accessed 20 July 2023)

Nickerson Family Association (2023) *Chatham, The Turning Point: The Mayflower and the Nickersons.* www.nickersonassoc.com (Accessed 20 July 2023)

Historic Chatham (2023) *The Mayflower Story.* www.historic-chatham.org (Accessed 21 July 2023)

Chapter 7

Good Reads (2023). *John F. Kennedy.* www.goodreads.com/quotes (Accessed 22 July 2023)

ThoughtCo. (2023) *How Rhode Island Colony Was Founded.* www.thoughtco.com/rhode-island-colony-103880 (Accessed 24 July 2023)

Newport Harbor Walk. (2023) www.cliffwalk.com (Accessed 24 July 2023)

Sherwood, Harriet. (2023) *"Anglicans reject Justin Welby as head of global church amid anger at same-sex blessings"* The Guardian, www.theguardian.com (Accessed 24 July 2023)

Christian Concern (2023) *Magna Carta and Church Freedom in a World of Lockdown.* www.christianconcern.com (Accessed 25 July 2023)

John F. Kennedy Presidential Library and Museum. (2023) *President's Remarks on Four Freedom.* www.jfklibrary.org (Accessed 25 July 2023)

Chapter 8

Good Reads (2023). *Martin Luther King Jr.* www.goodreads.com/quotes (Accessed 22 July 2023)

Long Beach New York. (2023) *Long Beach New York–The City by the Sea.* www.longbeachny.gov (Accessed 26 July 2023)

Hill Faith. (2021) *Apologetics.* www.hillfaith.org (Accessed 26 July 2023)

Good Reads (2023). *Eric Liddell.* www.goodreads.com/quotes (Accessed 22 July 2023)

Stanford University. (2023) *Parks, Rosa.* www.kinginstitute.stanford.edu/parks-rosa (Accessed 27 July 2023)

Chapter 9

Good Reads (2023). *John Lennon.* www.goodreads.com/quotes (Accessed 22 July 2023)

Tara Ross. (2023) *Americana.* www.taraross.com (Accessed 1 August 2023)

VINnews. (2023) *A Yom Kippur War Miracle.* www.vinnews.com (Accessed 1 August 2023)

Chapter 10

Good Reads (2023). *George Washington.* www.goodreads.com/quotes (Accessed 22 July 2023)

Christianity. (2023) *What does the Bible say about being deceived?* www.christianity.com (Accessed 2 August 2023)

End Times Bible Prophecy. (2022) *Deception in the End Times* www.end-times-bible-prophecy.com (Accessed 2 August 2023)

IMDB. (1983) *National Lampoon's Vacation.* www.imdb.com/title/tt0085995/fullcredits (Accessed 21 August 2023)

Good Reads (2023). *Phaedrus.* www.goodreads.com/quotes (Accessed 22 July 2023)

Lewis, C.S. (2009) The Lion, the Witch and the Wardrobe. 2nd Edition. Glasgow, HarperCollins.

Chapter 11

Good Reads (2023). *Thomas Jefferson.* www.goodreads.com/quotes (Accessed 22 July 2023)

National Park Service. (2022) *Historic Jamestowne* www.nps.gov (Accessed 3 August 2023)

The Culture Trip. (2023) *A Brief History of Colonial Williamsburg, Virginia* www.theculturetrip.com (Accessed 3 August 2023)

National Park Service. (2022) *Yorktown Battlefield* www.nps.gov (Accessed 3 August 2023)

Wikipedia. (2023) *Bruton Parish Church.* www.en.wikipedia.org/wiki/Bruton_Parish_Church (Accessed 4 August 2023)

Military. (2023) *The History of the Fourth of July.* www.military.com (Accessed 4 August 2023)

Chapter 12

Lyrics STANDS4 LLC. (2023) *"Country Road"* Kobalt Music Publishing Ltd/ Bill Danoff, John Denver, Taffy Nivert Danoff. www.lyrics.com/lyric/15992023/John+Denver/Country+Roads (Accessed 22 August 2023)

IMDB. (2007) *Evan Almighty.* www.imdb.com/title/tt0413099 (Accessed 21 August 2023)

Chapter 13

National Park Service. (2022) *Cape Henry Memorial* www.nps.gov (Accessed 5 August 2023)

National Park Service. (2022) *The Reverend Robert Hunt: The First Chaplain at Jamestown* www.nps.gov (Accessed 5 August 2023)

Claynash. (2023) *Pilgrim's Declaration* www.claynash.org (Accessed 5 August 2023)

The Filling Station. (2023) *Informal Expressions of the Christian Faith* www.thefillingstation.org (Accessed 5 August 2023)

Military Bases. (2023) *Fort Story* www.militarybases.us (Accessed 5 August 2023)

National Park Service. (2022) *Cape Henry Memorial Cross* www.nps.gov (Accessed 5 August 2023)

Chapter 14

Good Reads (2023). *Samuel Adams.* www.goodreads.com/quotes
(Accessed 22 July 2023)

Britannica. (2023) *Boston Tea Party* www.britannica.com/event/Boston-Tea-Party (Accessed 6 August 2023)

Discerning History. (2021) *William Brewster: Patriarch of the Pilgrims* www.discerninghistory.com (Accessed 6 August 2023)

Chapter 15

Plymrock. (2023) *Plymouth Rock Foundation* www.plymrock.org (Accessed 6 August 2023)

Chapter 18

Divine Hymns. (2023) *"I hear the sound of rustling"* Thank you Music/ Ronnie Wilson Morley. www.divinehymns.com/lyrics/i-hear-the-sound-of-rustling-song-lyrics (Accessed 22 August 2023)